TRADING

This Book Includes:"Options Trading Strategies + Trading Options". A Beginners Guide for Online Trading in Stock Market for Strategies with Passive Income and more...

By Michael Swing

Text Copyright © [Michael Swing]

Legal & Disclaimer

The information contained in this book and its contents is not designed to replace or take the place of any form of medical or professional advice; and is not meant to replace the need for independent medical, financial, legal or other professional advice or services, as may be required. The content and information in this book has been provided for educational and entertainment purposes only.

The content and information contained in this book has been compiled from sources deemed reliable, and it is accurate to the best of the Author's knowledge, information and belief. However, the Author cannot guarantee its accuracy and validity and cannot be held liable for any errors and/or omissions. Further, changes are periodically made to this book as and when needed. Where appropriate and/or necessary, you must consult a professional (including but not limited to your doctor, attorney, financial advisor or such other professional advisor) before using any of the suggested remedies, techniques, or information in this book.

Upon using the contents and information contained in this book, you agree to hold harmless the Author from and against any damages, costs, and expenses, including any legal fees potentially resulting from the application of any of the information provided by this book. This disclaimer applies to any loss, damages or injury caused by the use and application, whether directly or indirectly, of any advice or information presented, whether for breach of contract, tort, negligence, personal injury, criminal intent, or under any other cause of action.

You agree to accept all risks of using the information presented inside this book.

You agree that by continuing to read this book, where appropriate and/or necessary, you shall consult a professional (including but not limited to your doctor, attorney, or financial advisor or such other advisor as needed) before using any of the suggested remedies, techniques, or information in this book.

Table of Contents

OPTIONS TRADING STRATEGIES

Introduction _____ 21

How Options Work 25

Reading The Options Table 30

Rolling positions.. 36

1. How to Roll a Covered Call 38

2. How to Roll the Short Strangle... 43

3. Rolling a Short Call Spread 45

4. Rolling Short Put Spreads – cash secured 48

5. Rolling out a Butterfly Position 50

6. Adjusting a Butterfly to a Condor 52

Chapter 2: Strategic Planning for Options Trading 54

What is Strategic Planning... 54

Benefits it Offers 56

It allows you to be proactive 57

It gives you a sense of direction 57

Tips to Develop a Strategic Plan... 58

Chapter 3: Understanding the Greeks 61

The relevance of The Gamma... 62

Step-by-step Entry Guide 65

Portfolio Balance 65

Implied Volatility Percentile.. 67

Picking a Strategy 68

Strikes & Month 68

Position Size.. 69

Future Moves 70

Fundamentals of Options Strategies 71

Long calls 71

Short Calls 72

Long puts 72

Short puts 73

Selecting your strike price 73

Bullish options strategies.. 74

Bearish options strategies 74

Chapter 4: Choosing a Brokerage Account 75

The Importance of Choosing the Right Broker 75

Important Broker Qualities 77

The Standard of the Trading Software... 78

Simplicity of Order Entry and Transmission Speed 79

Quality of Service 80

Timely Executions and Confirmations... 82

Framework Capacity 82

Commission Costs 83

Customer Support.. 84

Order Execution Backups.. 84

Security of Individual and Financial Data 85

Best Brokers Specifically for Options Trading 85

E-Trade's 86

TD Ameritrade 86

Interactive Brokers 87

Charles Schwab 87

Ally 87

Trade Station 88

Fidelity 88

Tasty works 89

E Options 89

Creating a Backup Plan 89

Remaining Cautious with Brokers 92

Chapter 5: Making Short-term Trading Work 94

Straddling 97

Moving Averages 103

Cycles and Patterns 105

Chapter 6: Options Trading in the Forex Market 108

Chapter 7: The Option Pricing Models 123

Chapter 8: Fundamental Analysis 133

Fundamental Analysis Rules 134

Quantitative Fundamental Analysis 139

Important statements ....

Qualitative Fundamental Analysis 143

Chapter 9: Technical Indicators 145

Chapter 10: Open Interests in Options Trading 162

Chapter 11: Ensuring the Benefits Outweigh the Risks 166

Benefits 167

Maximizing Your Advantages 170

Reducing Your Risks 173

Chapter 12: Avoiding Common Mistakes 176

Buying cheap call options 177

No plan 181

Illiquidity 183

Conclusion 186

TRADING OPTIONS

Introduction 198

How Online Trading Works 199

Types of Online Trading 201

Online Trading to Gambling 202

3 Effects of the Addiction to the Friends and Family of the Online Trader 211

Chapter 1: What is finance marketing 214

What Is An Option? 214

The Concepts Behind Options 228

Chapter 2: Basics of stock market 233

Chapter 3: Technical and fundamental analysis 239

Technical analysis 239

Moving averages 240

Forex hedging against inflation 241

Bollinger bands 241

Fibonacci retracements 243

Stochastic oscillator 243

Sentimental analysis 244

Fundamental analysis 244

Employment 245

Weather conditions 246

GDP 246

Interest rates 247

Prices of commodities 247

Chapter 4: Trading Strategies for different asset classes 249

Why Do You Need a Plan? 249

Three Types of Strategies 253

Trading Strategies 254

Money-Management Strategies 256

Analysis and Improvement Strategies 258

Elements of Binary Options Strategies 259

Step 1 – Create signals 259

Step 2 – How much should you trade? 263

Step 3 – Improve your strategy 266

Strategies 269

Trend strategy 269

Pinocchio Strategy 270

Straddle Strategy 270

Risk-reduction strategy 271

Hedging strategy 272

Basic analysis 272

Chapter 5: Starting Forex Trading 274

Basics of Forex Trading 292

Forex Trading Tools and Strategies 304

Chapter 6: How to Avoid Costly Mistakes 320

Pricing Principles 322

In Action 331

Writing A Put Option 331

The Process of Writing A Call Option for Income 337

Chapter 7: Trading Tips for Intermediate Traders 345

1. Trading Forex Options Tips for Intermediate Traders 345

2. Tips for Intermediate Futures Options Traders 351

Chapter 8: Dos and Don'ts of Forex Trading **358**

Dos of forex trading 358

Research 358

Terminologies 359

Gain ratio 359

Strategies 360

Software 361

Calculate loss 361

Operation 362

Firm head on shoulders 362

Fundamental and technical analysis 363

Don'ts of forex trading 363

No planning 363

Short selling 364

Relying too much 364

Depending on luck 365

Picking extremes 365

Getting emotional 366

Expecting too much 366

Conclusion **368**

OPTIONS TRADING STRATEGIES

A step by step guide for online trading in stock market and foreign exchange whit great ideas analysis and strategies for passive income plan whit an ultimate trading flatforms thats can have best outcome

[Michael Swing]

Legal & Disclaimer

this book as and when needed. Where appropriate and/or necessary, you must consult a professional (including but not limited to your doctor, attorney, financial advisor or such other professional advisor) before using any of the suggested remedies, techniques, or information in this book.

Upon using the contents and information contained in this book, you agree to hold harmless the Author from and against any damages, costs, and expenses, including any legal fees potentially resulting from the application of any of the information provided by this book. This disclaimer applies to any loss, damages or injury caused by the use and application, whether directly or indirectly, of any advice or information presented, whether for breach of contract, tort, negligence, personal injury, criminal intent, or under any other cause of action.

You agree to accept all risks of using the information presented inside this book.

You agree that by continuing to read this book, where appropriate and/or necessary, you shall consult a professional (including but not limited to your doctor, attorney, or financial advisor or such other advisor as needed) before using any of the suggested remedies, techniques, or information in this book.

Introduction

A lot of investors only know about bonds, stocks, and mutual funds. Actually, there are so many types of investments that investors can put their money into. An option is one type of investment which offers a different kind of opportunity to experienced investors.

An option is very versatile because it allows an investor to adjust or adapt his position depending on the present situation. It can be conservative or speculative depending on the investing style of the investor. It means that he can protect his position depending on the market movement. However, the versatility of an option has its downside. An option is very complex and very risky. As such, a disclaimer is often issued by brokers when an investor wants to try options trading. Therefore, only serious investors are encouraged to try it. He must spend time studying options before he tries trading them. Thus, this book is a good start to learn about the trade.

An option is actually an agreement between the buyer and seller. The buyer is under no obligation to transact the underlying asset before the option expiry at a specific price. However, he has the right to demand the completion of the agreement. An option is a binding contract with strict definition of properties and terms. It a type of derivatives with an index or stock as the most common underlying asset used.

Types of Options

There are 2 kinds of options: call and put. A call option is a contract which provides the buyer the right to buy an underlying asset before it expires at a pre-agreed price. In stock trading, a call is like taking a long position. In this contract, the buyer is hoping that the price of the underlying asset will increase before the call option expires. A put option, on the other hand, is a right to sell an underlying asset before the contract expires and at a specific price. In stock trading, this is equivalent to taking a short position. A buyer of a put option hopes that the price of the asset goes down before the option expires.

Options can also be American or European. An American option is an option which can be exercised even before it expires. In general, an exchange-traded option is an American option. A European option is an option which can only be exercised on the date of expiration. A long term option is known as LEAPS or long term equity anticipation security. In terms of managing and controlling risk, LEAPS is similar to a regular option. However, LEAPS offer opportunities for a longer time. An exotic option is a non-standard option.

Stakeholders in an Options Market

There are 4 types of traders in an options market: buyer of call option, seller of call option, buyer of put option, and seller of put option. A person who purchases an option is called a holder while the one who sells it is called a writer. Just like in stocks, an investor who buys an option takes a long position while the one who sells it takes a short position.

In both options, a holder has no obligation to consummate the option contract. However, he has the right to either buy or sell the underlying asset if he wants to. Furthermore, a writer has an obligation to deliver his promise to either buy or sell the underlying asset if the holder exercises his right.

The Terminologies in Options Trading

The strike price is the price of the underlying asset which can either be sold or purchased. If it's a call option, the holder will make a profit when the market price of the underlying assets goes above the strike price. He can exercise the option if he wants to realize the profit. Otherwise, he can let it expire. On the other hand, if it's a put option, the writer will make a profit if the market price falls below the strike price. He can exercise the option if he wants to take advantage of the profit.

A listed option is an option which is traded through an options exchange. In the United States of America, options trader uses the Chicago Board Options Exchange to trade options. A listed option has an expiration date and a fixed strike price. Furthermore, 1 contract constitutes 100 shares of the underlying asset.

A call option is said to be "in the money" if the market price is above the strike price. In a put option, "in the money" means that the market price of the underlying asset is below the strike price. Intrinsic value is the "in the money" amount. The premium is the price paid for the option. It includes factors like volatility, strike price, market price of the underlying asset, and the time value of the option prior to expiration. The process of computing the option premium is very complex.

How Options Work

Why Trade Options

An investor can use options either to hedge or to speculate. In options trading, an investor can make a profit even if the market is down. In fact, he can even make money if the market moves sideways. This is the type of versatility that option trading offers.

Speculation is a trading strategy wherein a person can earn or lose a lot of money. It is because of this that trading options is considered very risky. If an investor buys an option, he has to correctly determine the time, the magnitude, and the direction of the underlying asset's price. He must be able to predict correctly the direction of the price. He must be correct about the time frame and the amount of change in the price. Plus, he has to consider that he has to pay commissions to the broker. As such, the investor has to beat all these odds in order to make money. He uses leveraging to earn a great deal of money.

Hedging is like insurance. He insures his investments in case their values fall. Large institutions actually use hedging because these establishments find it useful. Even an individual person can take advantage of hedging opportunities offered by the options market. For example, he wants to invest in technology stocks. However, he doesn't want to lose a lot of money from his stock investment. Thus, he can use options in order to limit his losses while taking advantage of the full opportunity offered by the technology stocks.

A third reason, although not available to everyone, allows a lot of companies to entice and keep their best employees through an employee stock option, which is similar to a regular option which provides the right to the holder to buy the company stock. The contract is between the company and its employee. In a regular option, the contract can be any two parties.

How Option Trading Works

For example, Company A has a stock price of $50 and a premium of $3.15 on May 1 for a July 53 Call. This means that the expiry date is on the **3rd** Friday of July and the strike price is $53. The contract price is $315 ($3.15 x 100 shares). Commissions are ignored in this example although in reality, the trader has to account for commissions.

The trader hopes that the stock rise will go up above $53 so that he'll make a profit. The break-even price for this contract is $53.15. The option is worthless when the stock price is $50 because it's less than the strike price of $53. After 2 weeks, the stock price went up to $61. The options contract is now worth $825. The profit will be $510 ($825 - $315). Therefore, in just 2 weeks, the investor is able to double his money. He can close his position by selling his option so that he can realize his profits or he can maintain his position if he thinks that the stock price will still go up. If at expiry date the stock price falls to $45, he can let it expire worthless and lose his original investment of $315 because the stock price is less than the strike price.

In reality, just 10% of these options are exercised. 30% of options are left to expire worthless and the rest is traded out. Holders of options sell their positions before expiry and the writers by them to close their positions.

In the example, the option premium increased from $3.15 to $8.25. Time value and intrinsic value made it possible for the premium to increase. Basically, the premium is the sum of the time value and intrinsic value. Intrinsic value is the in-the-money amount. In a call option, it is that point where the strike price is equal to the stock price. The time value, on the other hand, is the possibility that the option will increase in value. Therefore, in the example, the $8 is the intrinsic value while $0.25 is the time value. In general, an option always trade more than the underlying asset's intrinsic value.

Where to Buy Options

In the United States of America, options contracts are traded in different options exchanges. A trader must sign up with an options broker to be able to trade options. The orders to the broker are then routed to the options exchange. There are brokers who allow the trader to choose where to route his order while most brokers have their standardized way of choosing the exchange where the order is carried out.

Before trading options, the broker will first have to approve the trader's level of options trading. The trader has to fill out an options form which is used by the broker to evaluate the trading strategies as well as the level of understanding of options of the trader. In addition, the trader's general experience on investing is also evaluated. A broker has at most 5 levels of approval and includes factors like account balance, investing history, and investing objectives.

A trader's level may be conservative or aggressive. He is given options strategies by the broker depending on his options trading level. He may not be allowed to use riskier strategies if these involve a lot of risk. An experience trader with more liquid assets may be assigned a higher approval level than a person with a smaller account and less experience. After assigning an options trading level, the trader can start using the trading platform offered by the broker. He can start scanning positions which fit his trading strategy or market outlook. He can start submitting orders through the trading platform or through the phone.

There are less popular ways of routing orders. An over-the-counter option isn't transacted in an exchange. It is a contract between 2 independent parties. The disadvantage of an over-the-counter option is that it isn't regulated by the Options Clearing Corporation unlike the exchange-traded options. In general, only investors with large investments and institutional traders use over-the-counter options.

Reading The Options Table

Because of data dissemination and electronic trading, more and more traders are taking advantage of the benefits of trading options. Some use options to hedge while some traders try to speculate on the direction of the market price. There are also those traders who are still in the process of learning how to profit from the trade. Whatever their reason, they can be successful if they choose the right option. Currently, an option trader has a lot of resources available to him unlike traders in the past.

In previous years, newspapers report option price by a list of rows which is difficult to decipher. Today, some newspapers still use that old format of reporting option data. The reports usually consisted of notations like "P" or "C" to indicate a put or a call option. It also includes the last option trade price and the strike price. Some lists include open interest and volume figures. These figures are considered passé by most savvy option traders who understand various factors that can move options trading.

Today, options traders rely on online sources for option data. Although most sources have their own formats in the presentation of data, there are important variables that are present in each of the report. The OpSym in the first column of most reports include the symbol of the underlying asset, the contract month and year, the strike price, as well as the "p" or "c" notation to indicate a put or call option. The second column is the "bid" price, which is the most recent price a market maker offers to purchase a specific option. It means that a writer can make an order to sell a particular option contract at its bid price. The 3rd column is the ask price which is the most recent price a holder can buy a particular option contract.

It is important to note that market makers earn a living from the "bid" and "ask" prices. An option trader must compute the difference between the 2 prices before he considers entering or exiting a position. Usually, if the option is actively traded, it has a tighter spread (the difference between the bid and ask prices which is also the market maker's commission). If the spread is wide, it can cause a lot of problems to the short term trader because he can lose money even if he makes a profit.

The fourth column is the extrinsic bid/ask, which is the time premium that the option price has currently built. This information is important because ultimately all options lose their time premium at expiry date. The **5th** column is the implied volatility bid/ask. It is computed using a pricing model like the Black-Scholes model. It is the expected level of future volatility based on the option's current price and other variables used in computing volatility. A high implied volatility means that the option price has built more time premium. If the option trader can avail of historical implied volatility values, he can find out if the present extrinsic value is on a high or low level. If the extrinsic value is on a high level, the option is best for sellers. On the other hand, if it's low, it means that buyers can benefit most from the option.

The sixth column is the delta bid/ask, which is computed using a pricing model and represents the equivalent position of the underlying asset. The value can range from 0 to 100 for a call option and 0 to -100 for a put option. For example, if the delta is computed to be 50, it means that the risk/reward of the call option is the same as owning 50 shares of the underlying asset. If the underlying asset goes up by 1 point, the option can rise about 0.5 point. If the delta value is near 100, it means that the option is trading more like its underlying stock. The gamma bid/ask is on the 7th column. The value is also derived using a pricing model. It shows the number of deltas an option can gain or lose if the underlying stock gains a point. For example, a holder has a March 2015 125 call at $3.50. The delta will be 58.20, which means that if the value of the underlying stock goes up by $1 the option will gain about $0.5820. If the gamma value is computed to be 5.65 deltas, the delta will be 63.85 (58.20 + 5.65). This means that if the price of the underlying asset goes up by $1, the option gain will be about $0.6385.

The eighth column is the Vega bid/ask, which shows the amount that the option price can possibly rise or fall based on a 1 point increase in implied volatility. If the implied volatility goes up by a point, then in the example above the option price will gain $0.141. It is better to purchase an option if it has low implied volatility. On the other hand, it is better to sell an option if it has high implied volatility. The 9th column is the theta bid/ask, which the amount by which the option may fall due to the passage of a day. Because as was noted in the 4th column, as the option nears expiration, it loses it time premium. Furthermore, as the expiration draws near, the option loses it time value faster.

The tenth column is the volume which shows the number of contracts trader for the specific option as per the latest session. In general, a high volume option has a tighter bid/ask spread. The 11**th** column is the open interest which shows the number of open contracts of a specific option. The last column is the strike price, which the option price a buyer can pay for the underlying asset if he decides to exercise the option. It is also the price the seller will sell the underlying asset if the option is exercised by his buyer.

A call option has a higher option price if the strike price is lower. On the other hand, a put option is more expensive if the strike price is higher. Furthermore, a cap option has a positive delta while a put option has a negative delta.

Chapter 1: Managing Option Positions

Rolling positions

What is rolling?

Sometimes options traders wish to make adjustments to positions they hold in the market. When this happens, it means the trader's market outlook has changed. It is actually possible to roll a short or long option position.

The term rolling refers to changing the outlook on the underlying security of an option. This change is often driven by a change in the outlook of the markets and positions held on certain trades. In such situations, a trader is often worried that certain positions will be assigned.

Rolling is similar to making a different turn other than the one initially planned. Think, for instance, you leave home heading to the grocery store only to end up at the movies. This is very similar to what rolling is about.

The aim of rolling is to either deter or cancel the assignment. Basically, managing positions through rolling is an advanced technique that should only be applied by seasoned traders and experienced investors. Therefore, as an intermediate trader, you need to ensure that you thoroughly understand this process before applying it.

Rolling a position

Anytime that a trader rolls a position, he or she will be purchasing options very close to a current position in the marketing then sell this position in order to start another one. This process will cause small, minute but significant tweaks to the strike prices of options held by the trader. The effect of this move will be to shift the expiration times further out, so positions do not expire as initially planned. Even then, this process is not a guarantee that the strategy will work. In extreme cases, rolling will only compound losses, so it is advisable that only experienced traders apply this technique.

1. How to Roll a Covered Call

When you hold covered calls, you can choose to sell them in order to reduce the cost of holding them in long positions. When rolling calls forward, you will improve the break-even position and make it easier to be successful in the long run. However, you need to know if a position should be rolled on and when to do so. For instance, should rolling of a position occur 20 days to expiration or possibly at expiration?

Also, just about any trader can write a covered call. The most crucial thing is to manage such a position appropriately. Certain factors should be considered when rolling a position especially near expiration Fridays.

First, you need to confirm whether the underlying stock is suitable for this kind of management. Then you will need to confirm the option chains for statistics involving current and next month.

Now use the Ellman Calculator and enter the statistics in order to determine whether the dates are viable for rolling management. The 1-month goal for initial returns stands at 2% to 4%. With this information, you will finally need to conduct a thorough evaluation chart technical information and the prevailing market conditions. This way, you will comfortably be able to make adjustments to your trades to benefit more.

Example

Take the example where you invest in ABC stock at a price of $53 per share. You invest in this particular stock in the hope that the price will rise albeit modestly. At the same time, you wish to sell a 60-day covered call of ABC stock at a price of $55 per share. However, within a few days, you get to find out through a news item that ABC stock has good prospects in the long term.

This information changes your outlook so that you are now of the opinion that the stock price could actually rise to about $70 per share within six months. This catches your interest because your initial estimate about the profitability of ABC stock has increased exponentially. In such circumstances, there are a couple of things that you could do.

This is a clear demonstration of how a covered call with set positions and initial forecasts can go through some changes. It also could be that the initial forecast was wrong. As such, you have some options, and you can take action. Rolling action can help you switch your strategy and have a different approach.

Now if the stock price increases and you have no intention of selling the stock, then you will need better management skills as well as high assignment risks simply because the covered call that you have is now in the money. As such, you choose to purchase all your covered calls in order to cancel out any obligation to sell the stock. It is advisable at this stage to then sell a call option that has little chance of being assigned at a better strike price.

The common strategy when a stock forecast or objective changes is to adopt a rolling process. Rolling covered calls are usually adapted by seasoned traders. Even then, as a trader, you should understand that there is really no specific formula about the implementation of a rolling plan. For instance, as a trader, you may be wondering the current covered call should be shut down and replaced with yet another call that is in line with the new changes. If the answer is yes, will you prefer a covered call with a further expiration date and higher strike price compared to the previous call? There is generally not a correct or wrong solution and what you think is the best approach, should do. This is why experts say that covered call rolling is a decision that is subjective, and all investors and traders should take it into consideration in an individual and careful manner.

Rolling up a covered call

The process of rolling up a strategy like a covered call, for instance, entails buying out a position as well as closing existing covered call options. At the same time, you will sell a covered call with a higher strike price but similar expiration dates and the same underlying stock.

Rolling example

Our previous situation had the stock ABC at a price per share of $79. In this instance, the trader thinks the stock will trade within a confined range in the coming two months. As such, the trader decides to create a covered position by selling 1 ABC Call at $80 and then this price suddenly moves to $83 so that the call option is now at $85. While there are costs involved in making the adjustments, the possible benefits are much higher in essence.

Initial covered call: ABC stock costs $79 and has an expiration period of 60 days till October. The first step in this instance is to create another covered call by purchasing ABC shares at a price of $79. The next step would be to sell ABC stock at $80 with each call selling at a price of $2.50.

2. How to Roll the Short Strangle

Rolling is the process of making adjustments to options strategies that a trader sets up. There are varied reasons why traders actually make adjustments to their trades. These include erroneous initial predictions, changing market positions, and news that will affect the performance of a stock.

Now on a strangle strategy you always have a negative delta on the put and a positive delta on the call option. Therefore, we can deduce that we have a neutral delta in this instance. A neutral delta is okay at the onset. However, if the position remains that way then you lose money. As a trader, your desire is to make money; therefore, when there is movement in the stock price you want this movement to be huge. As such you may use gamma which will ensure the price goes up. However, should the stock price remain constant without any movement then you will lose money.

The short strangle is sometimes considered by traders as a very risky strategy. However, as an experienced trader who knows what he is doing; this is not necessarily the case. Here is a look at some circumstances where risk is reduced by rolling action.

First of all, premium is considered rather rich. As it is, a short straddle requires a trader to sell a put option, and a call option based on an underlying option with similar expiration dates and strike price. The best ones are the ones that offer a very rich premium under near-the-money or at-the-money conditions.

Also, it is crucial that short straddles have expiration dates that are within one month or less. It is time decay that causes the value of options to decline. This is why short straddles should be limited to only short-term options. Time decay often happens extremely fast within the first month.

Traders should focus their eyes on the current price, and the strike price then note the relationship. It is advisable to close positions once it becomes practically possible. This should happen especially when positions begin to move in the money. It is always a great idea to close at a profit because time decay will affect the value of the trade.

Also, keep a lookout for time decay. Therefore, once it begins to occur, you should plan to close the positions entered. Also, it is advisable to consider duplicating the strategy should the intrinsic value advance too fast. The forward movement in some instance can be unavoidable depending on certain factors such as price movement direction. In short, the price of the stock will not be volatile and as such time decay could have a positive effect on the two sides.

3. Rolling a Short Call Spread

When you roll a spread, the action is similar to rolling a single option. A trader who rolls a short call spread is most probably exit a position in a timely fashion with the strike prices moving down or up. The difference between rolling the short call spread and an individual option is that with the short call spread you will be engaged in a four-way trade. You will essentially be trading four different options instead of the usual two. This means opening two new positions while closing two existing ones.

Example

Let's say you have ABC stock that is trading at a price of $53. After a while, you begin to have bearish thoughts about this stock believing that the price will eventually go down. As such, you choose to sell a 30-day short call spread at 55/60. For this, you receive $1 per contract.

After some time, you realize that your prediction was wrong, and the price of ABC stock was not going to go down. The stock, instead of acting bearish suddenly turns bullish. ABC stock suddenly moves from the initial price of $53 to a short-term price of $55. At this juncture, your short call spread still has 15 days left to expiration. If you are to buy back the option, it would cost you $1.80 per contract. In this instance, you may choose to believe your initial forecast or follow the current trend.

If you choose to follow your initial analysis, then you may need to roll the strategy. When you do so, you will roll the expiration time out further and increase the strike price. As such, you will need to buy back at $1.80 the call spreads you sold at $1. You will then sell a short call spread with 45 days till expiration, a long strike price of $65 and a shirt strike price of $60. You will sell these options are a price of $1.10 per contract.

At the start of this position, you were $0.80 down because of selling the options $1 and buying at $1.80. However, after the rolling process, should the ABC stock price be below $60 at the prevailing expiration date, then you will be ahead with the $0.30. You should hope that all your analysis was correct and that this stock will expire below the $60 mark. This way, you will end the trade at a profit. However, should this not happen, then you will begin incurring losses pretty fast.

Basically, if you implement a roll process on a stock option position, be careful not to compound your losses because this is something that is quite possible. Therefore, if you are confident about your initial predictions, you should try and stick to your game plan. Alternatively, you could choose to exit the strategy rather than roll and incur even larger losses.

This particular roll management process applies to most two-legged trades and not just the short spreads. Rolling also applies to other formations including back spreads and straddles.

4. Rolling Short Put Spreads – cash secured

Let us use an example to understand how this roll operation works. Let us assume that you have sold a cash-secured put option with underlying stock ABC at a strike price of $50. During the process, you sold some put options and received $0.9 per contract even as ABC price at the time was $51. After some time, the price of ABC stock dropped to $48.5 as it approaches expiration.

Some of the few options that you have as a trader include purchasing back some of the options that you sold. As such you will buy back options with the strike price of $50 before these are reassigned. The major challenge now is that you will buy back the options at a price of $1.55 even though you purchased the same at a price of $0.90.

There are several tools that you can use when rolling the call. One of these is making use of Ally Invest spread order screen. When you use this screen, you will notice that you can actually buy the $50 strike price option. As you execute this trade, you will also sell options with a $47.50 price which is an actual roll down of the strategy. This will have a 90-day expiration period, and the cost per trade is $1.70. As such, you will receive a net credit of $15 for 100 share contracts at $0.15.

The example above indicates clearly how you can roll out and actually save yourself from an impending loss or improve an existing position. There will also be a significant increase in the time value which is crucial after obtaining the 90-day option.

Let us assume that put with the $47.50 strike price goes on to expire worthless after a period of 90 days then you will gain $1.05 per each. This will eventually earn you $105 per contract. Even then, you need to take precaution because you could be taking a loss every time you roll down. Also, you should secure any gains that you make in the market. When you do not, then you risk compounding your losses. This kind of risk is not worth it so always take precaution when rolling out positions.

Always make sure that you roll out within the shortest time so as to face fewer risks in the market. Sometimes it may be necessary to incur some costs in order to roll out a position. Once a position than you have sold gets into the money, you will need to make a determination as to whether rolling is necessary. Basically, you need to think about rolling a position before it gains more than 2% to 4% in the money. This will also be based on other factors such as market conditions, volatility, and value of the stocks among others.

If you let a position get too much into the money, it will be difficult to end up in a profitable position. Also, think about what is known as a preemptive roll which basically dictates that you should implement any rollouts on positions before options get into the money. Do so if you think the position is headed that way. This lowers your rolling costs and makes it much better for you as a trader.

5. Rolling out a Butterfly Position

As a trader, you need to have a great trading plan that allows adjustments to positions that you have taken in the market. This is because markets and positions keep changing in the course of a trading period. Therefore it is advisable to work within a set of guidelines rather than a set of strict rules.

Butterfly trade example

Take the example of the ABC April 2016 put options butterfly strategy that was set up with a long call. The long call is initiated for hedging the upside of the trade. An unforeseen instance happened where the price of ABC stock went up steeply while the trade did not have a promising outlook.

After about a week's time, some adjustments became necessary. In our case above, the most appropriate solution was to initiate a rolling process. To do this effectively, it was determined that another butterfly position with a long call should be introduced. The initial butterfly is therefore rolled so that its outlook improves to avoid incurring unnecessary losses.

Making the adjustment is crucial because it helped save an otherwise desperation situation. As it is, such adjustments serve numerous purposes, but the best are those that allow trades to proceed to a conclusion and within desirable profit margins.

It is essential to note that the intervention described above as one that was not based on any rules and had not been initially planned. It was only designed and executed when the need arose and based on the needs at the time. This is basically how trades are supposed to be executed as well as intervention methods such as rolling. You will find that this kind of approach works best and helps to reduce risks and improve outlooks.

6. Adjusting a Butterfly to a Condor

As a trader, you may set up a butterfly position which may then experience certain challenges that may cost you significant losses. One of the options you may want to consider is turning the position from a butterfly to a condor. A butterfly spread can easily be split into two distinct spreads.

Ideally, you will want to split the original butterfly and create an additional butterfly. When you do this, you will come up with a condor. You will still have two spreads but with completely different sold strikes. At this juncture, you would not necessarily adjust the butterfly. However, the intervention is necessary especially when the price of the underlying stock was rising and while other indicators showed the option was headed towards a loss.

Making such adjustments is necessary especially where losses seem inevitable based on conditions, but the situation can be rescued. But the interventions should be designed and implemented based on market trends, conditions, volatility, price action, and other related factors.

Chapter 2: Strategic Planning for Options Trading

Strategic planning is an integral part of sustainable success, be it in business or in options trading. Let's talk about how to make a game plan for your trades in this chapter.

What is Strategic Planning

For starting a business, you need a blueprint, a plan. Without any direction or planning, nothing works. Options are the same way. To make great trades consistently, you need a solid strategic plan. On top of all this, options aren't simply buying something cheap and selling it at a higher price to make a profit. It's infinitely more complex than that. There are basically two types of options namely the call options and the put options, but they're simultaneously two kinds of strategies too. You purchase in one and sell in the other. It all depends on your inclination towards being bearish or bullish. But options wouldn't be complicated at all if there were just these two strategies.

Earlier in this book, it has been mentioned, that there are a lot of complex mathematical operations that have to be done to calculate and formulate a plethora of strategies. The basic ingredients of all these strategies are the two primary options namely the call and put options. The multitudes of strategies that are so formulated are the different permutations and combinations of these two and other things.

CBOE- Chicago Board of Options Exchange is the largest such exchange in the world, which offers options on a wide variety of single stocks, indexes, and ETFs. Traders can create multiple option strategies varying from buying or selling a single option to very complex and intricate ones that include multiple simultaneous option positions.

Benefits it Offers

To prevent your emotions from affecting the trade, a plan needs to be created. Experiencing the otherworldly happiness of making a huge gain or a heartbreaking amount of loss can make your mind spin, and you might deviate from the original strategy you had in mind if you had one, which you need to. Strategic planning helps you with that. It gives you detailed yet simplified instructions on specifically how to tackle every trading situation, should they arise. If you are following a well-formed strategy efficiently, you can even handle multiple trades. Thus, you don't need to skip a good opportunity if presented with it. However, taking up too many trades may expose you to too much risk. A well-structured trading strategy tells you both how you are making trades and the reason for which you're doing it.

Not only has that, but good strategic planning also guided you on how to monitor the results. One should know whether the strategy they're applying is working in the desired manner. Random trades where one just sells and buys for any reason which seems good, does not give any useful feedback, because the gains and losses will be as random as the impulses which made the trade. But by using strategic planning, the right amount calibrated adjustments can be made to the trading process to improve it overall.

It allows you to be proactive

When you have a plan, you can predict the future better and prepare accordingly. It helps you anticipate unfavorable scenarios and take the necessary actions to avoid negative impacts. This way, you are not just reacting to negative situations but are rather proactively avoiding them. Market trends are ever-changing, and if you want to stay on top of your game, you need always to be proactive to stay ahead of the competition.

It gives you a sense of direction

With a strategic plan, you get a bearing of where you currently stand and in what direction you need to go in order to achieve your goals and objectives. When your plan is in sync with your vision and goals, you go forward with that much energy. It also helps you make more efficient decisions and evaluate your success better.

Tips to Develop a Strategic Plan

Now that we've established the need for a strategic plan, we need to know about certain things to develop a strategic plan. Developing a strategic plan takes into consideration a lot of factors.

- **The amount of capital you have**
- **The type of capital you have**
- **Your inclination towards being a bull or a bear**
- **The existing conditions in the market**
- **Market volatility**
- **Technical environment**
- **Your affinity with risk**
- **Are you a long term or short-term investor?**

- **Your technical knowledge and expertise**

Now, this list is not exhaustive but covers a major chunk of all the things you need to take into consideration while developing a strategic plan. Coming to the tips to develop a strategic plan, just know that options are not like any other investments. They require deep analysis and detailed, methodical approaches. So, the first tip would be to see how much capital you have and then choose a strategic plan, which will work efficiently with the amount of capital you have. If you do not have a lot of capital, start with a short-term strategy, which generates profits early so you can gather some more capital and prepare yourself for a more intensive investment. However, with more profit potential comes more risk, and that's where your risk preference comes in. If you're a safe player who wants a stable income even though the rate is lower, then plan a strategy that gives you low but regular returns. If you're a risk taker, then you can aim for greater profits, but take note that you should ideally not invest in higher risk strategies with borrowed capital because the overall liability might increase. Invest in such strategies with your own money and profits, which do not have any inherent liabilities. Another tip would be to determine the direction you want to go with, whether it's going to be a bearish approach or bullish approach. But at the same time, another auxiliary tip would be, to be flexible with your approach. If your general trading style is inclined to the bearish side, but it's reasonably apparent that being a bull about now would be better, and vice versa, then being rigid is not good.

Chapter 3: Understanding the Greeks

When you think of the word "Greeks," the mighty Olympians may come to your mind, but we're studying options, aren't we? Now that we know what options are, it's time to move on to the options strategies. But is it? Before we do that, it is important to understand what the Greeks are and their relevance in affecting the price of every option you'll trade in. The examples being used here are hypothetical in nature and don't represent real-world scenarios.

An investment has a lot of risks, and through options, one can manage these risks. Minimal risk strategies are opted by conventional investors but to earn more profits, a lot of investors go for bolder strategies that involve more risk. And the thing about options is, one can measure and modify the risk of any stock market investment.

It is when you calculate the different risks, that a set of Greek letters, the group of which is known as 'The Greeks' are put in use to measure or express in certain quantifiable terms, the risks which one faces in an investment.

Now I know you might be wondering what Vega is doing here since it's not a Greek letter. Don't worry about that; it's inconsequential. What our real focus should be on is that by using the Greeks of a position, certain risk variables are measured and can be modified to bear the risk endurance of the investor. Let's start the introduction.

The relevance of The Gamma

Gamma is important because it has a direct effect on the one Greek that greatly determines the value of stock options most, which is the Delta. We know how delta changes now. But what is the quantity by which options Delta changes? Think of the Gamma as velocity. While speed is a scalar quantity, which measures only the magnitude, Gamma is the vector quantity, which means it measures the magnitude and the direction of the change.

The significance of Gamma is for directional and hedging trades.

- For Directional trades, to get an overall position, gamma needs to incline towards the direction of interest, so that option delta increases with the development of trade.

- For hedging trades, you would need as low gamma as possible on overall options to make sure the options trading position remains very neutral to changes in the underlying stock.

Options Gamma does not matter much when one is buying a call or put options for one a directional trade as one can be sure that they're already purchasing positive options gamma meaning that delta of your options will rise with a rise or fall in the stock.

Theta

Thus, we can say that Theta measures the everyday percentage of depreciation of a stock option's price with the underlying stock showing no change. It represents the rate of time decay of options.

It is directly proportional to the Gamma, which means more the gamma, more the theta. While an option is having high gamma return very high profits with stock price changes, but it has a higher theta too, which impairs the price of the option quickly.

But in case, no significant movement happens early, the option could lose substantial money. So, with an aggressive option position, you should also consider the high risk associated because of the higher options theta. The tradeoff needs to be favorable.

The theta is lower for OTM options than it is for ATM options because the dollar amount of time value is smaller.

Vega

A stock option has two main components related to price.

1. Intrinsic value

2. Extrinsic value

Vega does not affect the intrinsic value but affects the time value of an option's price. Thus, the longer-term options will have a higher Vega than shorter-term options.

Step-by-step Entry Guide

Before you start making any trades, there are certain things you should check. This is a strategic step-by-step guide that will help you pick great trades and filter out bad trades consistently. The order facilitates quickly figuring out whether a trade is worth your time.

Portfolio Balance

Portfolio balance is everything. So even before you begin looking for a new trade, you need to ask yourself how it will fit in your portfolio. You need to question whether you need the trade. If, for example, you already have a lot of bullish trades in your portfolio, you probably don't need another one.

Balancing out trades is the key to developing a good portfolio as it reduces risk. So, when you already have a handful of bullish trades, you should be looking for some bearish trades that will offset your risk. When you know what kind of trade you need to look for from the get-go, it helps you filter better and focus only on what your portfolio needs.

Liquidity

Liquidity is one of the most important factors when it comes to picking great, tradable stocks. An illiquid option is not worth your time. So, when looking for a new trade, you should follow this general rule of thumb: if the underlying stock trades approximately 100k shares daily, then it's good to go. Since it's a big and efficient market, we can be confident in the fact that the calculations will only become more accurate as time passes. For underlying options, if the strikes you are trading have at least 1000 open interest contracts, this is preferable. This makes sure you can get in and out of the market fast as it is liquid enough.

Implied Volatility Percentile

Once we've picked out the trades that pass the previous two criteria, the next step is to check whether the IV is relatively low or high. This is measured using IV percentiles. So, for example, if GOOG has IV of 40% but an IV percentile of 80%, this means that over the last year, more than 80% of the time the volatility would be lower than it currently is (40%). This implies that the implied volatility for GOOG is relatively high, meaning you should consider premium-selling strategies.

Similarly, if FB has an IV of 35% but an IV percentile of 30%, it means that over the last year, only 30% of the time the IV was lower than what it is currently (35%). This also implies that there is a 70% chance the IV will increase, so the IV is relatively low for FB and you should prefer to be a net buyer.

Picking a Strategy

When we talk about picking the best strategy, it is more about eliminating than selecting. Once you have a good grasp of how the underlying stock's IV and IV percentile affect the options, you can start eliminating strategies that wouldn't make sense here. For example, in case the option pricing is rich, and IV is high, we can eliminate strategies like calendars, long single options, debit spreads, etc. Then we can go ahead and select the best strategy from the ones left (credit spreads, strangles, iron condors, etc.) depending on our account size and risk tolerance.

Strikes & Month

Once you have selected the right strategy, the next step is to place trades at a probability level you're comfortable with. Say, you're going to be selling credit spreads below the market. You could sell your credit spreads at a strike price that gives you a 70% chance of success or a strike price that gives you a 90% chance of success. Both are high probability trades, but one is clearly more aggressive. You can pick either one if you're sure it fits your goals and your style. You also need to give yourself enough time to make sure the trade can work for you. For high IV strategies, you'd want to place them at 30-60 days out, and for low IV strategies, you'd want to go with 60-90 days. Why? Because the longer timeline boosts your theta value and counters the low volatility.

Position Size

One of the most crucial areas where many traders - even the experienced ones - fail is position sizing. Once you've gone through all the previous steps, you should carefully evaluate your position size before placing a trade. There have been numerous studies that have shown that your risk increases exponentially when trading big positions, and you could easily end up blowing up your whole account. This is why for beginners and intermediates I advise going with a small position at all times. Place all your trades on a sliding scale of 1-5% of your total balance. This is your risk scale.

How do you define risk? Simple, it's the cash or margin you put up to cover a trade. If you were to sell a $1 wide credit put spread for 25 cents, you would need to put up $75 margin to cover it. Now, if your account is worth $10,000, and for each trade, you wish to allocate 2% of your account, the $75 margin is what would be used to base the trade-off. So, you can take $200 of risk (2% of $10,000) divided by $75 per contract. This comes out at 2.66, which means you could sell 2.66 spreads at most.

To be safe, you should always round it down, never up.

Future Moves

Just like chess players need to be thinking a few moves ahead (at least the good ones do), a good trader also needs to be thinking ahead. You should always have a Plan B for when things go wrong, and this should mean more than just being able to shield yourself from a losing trade.

Although that is important, you should also be thinking about scenarios where the stock doesn't move, and you might have to roll it over to the next month. You need to know whether the options even exist for the next contract month. The stock might have earnings coming up soon, or a dividend might be paid out soon.

You need to remember that some trades **will** go wrong, as is the way of the market. If you're constantly asking yourself important questions, your brain stays alert and formulates new plans to adjust if the need arises.

Fundamentals of Options Strategies

Long calls

It is the simplest option strategy to learn about. That does not mean the profit-making is easy. It is a bullish strategy, but one must be right about many things to make it profitable. For that, a trader needs to be right about the direction of the stock price movement and the quantum of it. The time it takes to move must also be correct. Right on all these three elements makes the long call strategy profitable. The upside profit potential is unlimited but things like volatility and time erosion work against a long option.

Short Calls

These are not good for newbies in options trading. It is also called a naked call, as it is uncovered. It is quite a risky position because the upside risk here is unlimited and the profit is limited (happens when the stock price drops). Short Call Write is a credit strategy where you get money for putting on the position, which puts the broker at risk if you are not able to cover the position when required.

Long puts

Like a long call trade, a long-put trade is simple to understand. Put strategies are generally harder to make a profit in, but the strategy is a basic component of many complex options strategies. A long-put option is bearish in terms of inclination. With long calls, an investor needs to be right about the direction of stock price movement and the amount of it with the time frame to make a profit. The maximum potential loss on a long-put trade equals the price paid for the option. The profit potential, however, is quite substantial if the stock price drops.

Short puts

The short puts are not as risky as the short calls. But that in no way means that newbies in option trading can easily make profits using this strategy. When a put is sold, a profit/loss situation opposite to that of a long put is created. The profit, when the stock price rises, is limited to the premium received on selling the option. The downside risk keeps rising until the stock's value is zero. The margin requirements of this strategy are high, and thus, significant funds are required.

Selecting your strike price

Options traders often have a hard time determining the strike prices they are going to use. The type of strike price (ATM, OTM, and ITM) affects the quantum of the movement of the underlying asset price required to make a profit. Even if the underlying stock remains stagnant, profit can be made by using an appropriate strike price. The bearishness or the bullishness of the investor needs to be matched accordingly.

Bullish options strategies

If an investor is extremely bearish, out of the money long puts or in-the-money short calls should be considered. These require a highly bearish move of an equally high quantum in the underlying stock to become profitable. But if you're not that bearish, ITM long puts or OOTM short calls should be considered. OOTM can result in a profit sometimes, even when there's no price change in the underlying stock.

Bearish options strategies

Most option strategies have a higher profit potential when they need a substantial price movement in the underlying stock, but it's also less likely to make a profit. OOTM short puts and OOTM short calls can make a profit possible even with zero movement in the underlying stock. But they are extremely risky. Using credit spreads is a safer alternative but has less profit potential.

Chapter 4: Choosing a Brokerage Account

When selecting an online broker for your options trading, there's one essential principle- There is no replacement for options experience. Obviously, make your own decisions. Because somebody loves a broker does not mean you will—or that you need to utilize them.

What you need to do, in any case, is build up a plan for assessing the brokers you consider, so you will guarantee that the one you eventually pick offers the features you need—and certainly require.

The Importance of Choosing the Right Broker

Not all firms will have the capacity to give the affirmations you need regarding all your worries. The more things you need to consider with respect to the "mechanics" of online trading, the more opportunities will be made available for you to end up diverted and falter as you move along the way to options trading.

In case you are a genuinely new trader, you may likewise need to check whether the broker offers any close to home, one-on-one investment counsel, or proposes trading chances to customers. Relatively few online firms do, yet in the event that such things are important to you, it does not hurt to inquire. You may, at any rate, get a referral to a partnered warning service or data site that can help give some trading thoughts.

This enables a client to manage a prepared options broker to deal with orders and questions. The commission charges are not quite the same as the online rates—yet the value offered by having a live broker will most likely be worth the expense in case you are simply taking in the trading ropes.

Obviously, the essence of online trading is accomplishing direct access to the trades, so you can perform your transactions precisely like the experts. In this way, you should attempt to wean yourself from

the requirement for broker help before going online—
or as fast as possible from there on.

Important Broker Qualities

Choosing a good broker is crucial in order to make
sure all parts of your plan are implemented. A big
mistake that many traders make is not finding a
broker. This doesn't always mean going to some guy's
office, so he can tell you exactly what to do. There are
online brokers that don't tell you what to do in any
form. The decisions are left up to you and you have
the tools to make your own choices.

The biggest reason that traders don't want to get a
broker is because they aren't free. Some require a
payment up front, and most will take a commission
fee, meaning you won't always make as much from
your returns. Not everyone that trades has a broker,
but for a beginner, it's important to get some help
from one. Even if you manage to go through your first
few months without needing much of their advice, it's
still an insurance policy that can give you peace of
mind. While you might have to pay out a fee, it's much

better to give that money than to end up losing it all anyway.

The Standard of the Trading Software

For online traders, this is the most basic issue, and it takes various inquiries to decide exactly what number of features is incorporated—and how great they are. Is the software user-friendly; easy to comprehend and simple to utilize? Can I get it on a disk or would I be able to download it from the internet? Is it hard to install on my PC? Will I require help?

If you don't have access to such resources, you should check if it requires any unique equipment or communications highlights, for example, high-speed modems, specialty internet browsers or DSL lines—with the end goal to make it work proficiently. Check if it incorporates adequate pricing and logical, analytical tools for your requirements.

If it does not include these things, check if it is built to be effortlessly incorporated into independent quotation frameworks and analytical services. Is satisfactory customer documentation given—both printed and online—to enable both to understand the framework and manage any technical issues?

Another question to ask about the standard of the trading software is whether it is attractive to look at— and, in the event that you do not like it, would you be able to change such things as size or color or display? This may appear to be unimportant, yet in case you will be an active trader, you might take a look at it on and off for six or seven hours every day. Thus, you need to ensure that it is something that you do not end up hating.

Simplicity of Order Entry and Transmission Speed

The simplicity of order entry and transmission speed is additionally critical for active traders, who might put in heaps of requests and need the procedure to be as programmed as possible. Ask yourself: What number of fields on the order-entry screen do I need to fill in to put in a request? Determine if you need to type in all the data, or if the software imports it from the logical or pricing screens in the event that you need it to.

Do I need to manually go back to the firm's order screen, or would I be able to get to it by tapping on the screens given by incorporated trading partners? Does the program send the order to the trade when I submit it, or does it need to be prepared elsewhere inside the firm first? Do I need to indicate the trade where the order is sent, or does the program shop around at the best cost and course the order as need be?

You will want to determine if you have to put orders specifically through the software, or if you have a browser to get to your framework. Figure out if orders need to be entered at night-time, for execution the next day—or just while the market is open. Consider if you can also put orders from the site and also through the software.

Quality of Service

The quality of service is one important factor in determining if a brokerage is right for you. Start by asking: Are there independent order screens for stocks and options? If not, can the order screen be personalized to take into account options traders? Are the options quotes given in the order screen constantly or deferred?

In the event that you call up an option chain, determine if it is a real-time preview, or a delayed collation of last prices. Furthermore, explore if it is spread out in an orderly way, or if you must search for the option you need. Does the option-pricing framework give you access to current bids and offers, or simply last trading prices? What about volume numbers? Open interest?

Determine if the framework includes multi-option strategies, for example, spreads, and give you a chance to order them as a unit. If so, make sure it charges one commission for such orders—or survey fees for every option in the combination. Ask if the framework will settle for stop and stop-limit orders on options.

What about stops and buy orders that are dependent upon the price of the basic asset? Do any of the incorporated quote services specialize in options? If yes, will their program give me a chance to punch in trade parameters and screen for good trading chances? Does the brokerage firm's program have any comparable services to assist me with options analysis?

Timely Executions and Confirmations

The broker's order entry program ought to give guided access to the electronic trading frameworks of the suitable trades, and, once your trades qualify for programmed execution, report back a confirmation in few seconds—ideally to an area of the order-entry screen where you can quickly observe that you got your fill. In the event that the trade does not qualify the bill for programmed execution, it ought to show up in a corner on your screen intended to give you a chance to monitor your working orders.

Framework Capacity

The broker's database ought to have the adequate reserve processing capacity to deal with additional overwhelming order stream—and the firm ought to have a framework set up to manage quick economic situations as successfully as possible. (No firm is flawless when such circumstances occur, yet they should strive to make an attempt to at the very least—

not simply hurl their hands and say, "Sorry" or "Too bad!")

Commission Costs

Numerous traders would put commissions much higher on the list than other important quality factors; however, our reasoning is unique. What great are low commissions in the event that you get lousy prices, moderate executions and terrible (or no) benefit? Ensure the broker gives you all that you need—and require—and do not stress on the chance that it cost a couple of additional dollars.

You will likely influence it up on your trades, at any rate. Do, in any case, demand that the broker's fees, at any rate, be competitive; you need to pay for what you get—not pay to get gouged. Additionally, make sure to get some information about possibly precarious things covered up underneath a guarantee of low commissions—e.g., a commission rate of $1 per option would not help you a whole lot if the firm forces a $50 least on each order.

Customer Support

Very important! It's a must have—ideally by telephone, not only online, by email or through a self-improvement menu on the site (in spite of the fact that it's pleasant to have those choices too). Likewise, see if support is accessible simply amid business hours — or terribly, just when the market's open. Your goal is to guarantee that the help services will be accessible on the occasions you really require help.

Order Execution Backups

There might be times when things turn out badly—even with the best broker and the most superb programming. In the event that it occurs within trading hours, your broker must have a backup framework to manage it. That implies having enough telephone lines and in-house individuals to deal with client calls and the sudden flood of disconnected order stream.

All things considered, no trader who frantically needs to escape a position 30 minutes before the end wants to call his broker and hear a tinny, computer voice, "All agents are presently occupied; however, your call is vital to us. Please stay on the line; a delegate will be with you in roughly 45 minutes"— soon after you have lost your shirt!

Security of Individual and Financial Data

Numerous individuals fear to do anything online in light of the fact that they fear a hacker, or another person will discover about them, take their identity— or, more terribly, take their money. In substantial part, these fears are unreasonable—particularly inside the frameworks of America's financial services systems, which were planned in view of security and had unique assurances, set up. Therefore, most brokerage frameworks are as secure as it's presently conceivable to make them. All things considered, it never hurts to make an inquiry.

Best Brokers Specifically for Options Trading

Not all brokers operate in the same manner, so it's important to make sure you are finding one that will work with your methods of option trading. Some brokers specialize in penny stocks while others strictly work with options. While you might know someone that personally deals with a specific type, make sure you are still using a broker that has an extensive comprehension of options so that you can implement the best strategies.

The biggest flaw in any trader is inexperience. You might make the wrong investments here and there, or lose money that you could have expanded, but the main reason for this in the end is usually inexperience. If you are investing in a person that's specifically to combat this big mistake, you want to make sure they have a track record that proves their relevancy.

E-Trade's

Options House platform and mobile application are the highest quality levels of option trading platforms. Options House at present gives traders premium-quality tools without the top-notch price tag.

TD Ameritrade

This online broker compensates for higher-than-normal trading commissions with superior service, research, and trading tools that will make everybody from amateur investors to active traders upbeat. **This**

one is best for beginners and has the best options tools.

Interactive Brokers

Interactive Brokers is a solid option for cutting edge, frequent traders. The broker offers worldwide trade abilities, low commissions, and a quality trading platform. Be careful though, because new traders may be killed by inertia fees, high parity necessities and an absence of instructive assets.

Charles Schwab

Charles Schwab has earned its solid reputation. The broker offers top-notch client benefits, two powerful trading platforms and a wide range of commission-free ETFs and no-transaction-fee shared assets. **This option** is best for order types.

Ally

Ally is a vigorous trading platform and a line-up of free research, outlining, information and logical devices make it a decent decision for active traders. But on the other hand, it's proper for starting investors who will value that there is no minimum for the account and no yearly fees. This one is the best low-cost broker and can be **found here**.

Trade Station

Trade Station is the best quality website for trading active stock, futures and options. This brokerage is for investors who depend on the broker's high-octane trading platform, reams of research, and modern logical tools. The firm gives three commission plans including flat fee, per contract/per share and unbundled pricing plan. The absence of commission-free ETFs and common assets can be a turnoff to few investors. Overall, it's a well-rounded offering

Fidelity

Fidelity is a platform that shows traders the correct way to do things and gives them every resource they require as the trading goes. Options trading can be scary and confounding for new traders. Fidelity offers a huge collection of free research and information introduced in a way that is not overpowering for inexperienced traders. **This** is the best option for research and training.

Tasty works

Tasty works has become famous in options trading. The brokerage, driven by its parent financial media organization, Tasty Trade, offers probably the best rates in options trading matched with incredible tools and options for traders.

E Options

E Options gives a proficient, nitty-gritty platform for active investors who prefer low expenses to an extravagant platform. The investment funds can be critical for cutting-edge stock and options traders who have different sources for the research and information they require.

Creating a Backup Plan

Be absolutely mindful, nonetheless, that regardless of how good a brokerage firm is being painted, you will more than likely run into an issue or two while preceding before all is said and done. These could be the consequence of disturbances at the exchanges, with your broker's database, or with your own computer, internet connection, or telephone line.

You could even commit an exorbitant error as the consequence of stupid calculation errors. Approximately fourteen years back, we signed onto our internet browser to check the news and opening market indices —and nearly hopped into frenzy mode when the EarthLink™ start page showed the Dow down 397.85 for just 10 minutes after the opening.

Obviously, it was simply a terrible calculation error; the Dow was down simply 7.85—however, the browser's numbers were not right throughout the day. Had we followed up on those numbers, it could have been a catastrophe. Be that as it may, that is only the manner in which it is in today's powered-up world, kept running by PCs, encouraged by telephone lines and absolutely subject to the ideal execution of electrical transmission lines.

To shield yourself from the impacts of these mechanical caprices, build up a reinforcement plan that goes past simply hoping to get the telephone and call your broker when the framework goes down. Create a plan in which you are certain you generally have both limits as well as stops set up on your weak positions—both profitable and unprofitable.

Be certain you completely comprehend the risks before attempting new strategies or starting new plays. Print out day by day copies of your open positions in the event that the broker's server fails. Closely observing your account status, particularly your equity balance, and print hard copies of key account outlines at any rate week by week.

With those protections set up, technical issues may cost you a little loss. However, you will never confront an overwhelming financial difficulty. What's more, should the broker encounter a total framework disappointment, your paper duplicates will kill any plausibility of debate in regard to your positions and value of accounts.

These concerns are legitimate. However, they are not really motivations to shy away from options trading—particularly given the technological and innovative advancements.

Remaining Cautious with Brokers

One last admonition about picking a broker: Just because a sales representative or promotional material says a brokerage firm offers some new feature on their software or an exceptional service does not imply that it's quite true. As we know, some marketers are emissaries of frivolity, preferring to promote the positive and disregard the negative. In this manner, the cases you read delivered by the firms themselves might be painfully exaggerated.

In all truth, managers and programmers frequently tell advertisement marketing specialists that some new service or product highlight will be available when the promotion turns out, and then fail to meet their own schedule. What's more, sales representatives are every now and then told things that are non-existent work better than they do—and, not being experts and ready to decide for themselves, just pass the misrepresentations along.

Try to do more other than converse with the brokerage agent. Look at some reviews, online and in popular financial magazines, here and there. Then speak with people who have been in the industry for a very long time.

Chapter 5: Making Short-term Trading Work

Short-term options trading is an excellent pursuit for beginner options traders, but also, and perhaps surprisingly, for more experienced and seasoned options traders as well. In fact, short-term options are becoming more popular within the options world. "Weekly" options, in particular, have undergone a rather rapid growth in popularity in recent years, and seem to bring a substantial amount of success to those who decide to utilize them. For those still unsure about what a weekly option entails, it's essentially just an option that expires in one week. Typically, an asset is posted on Thursday, and expires that following Friday.

But aside from that, short-term options are also excellent trading pursuits because they decrease the financial risk associated with options. With short-term options trading, trades are handled relatively quickly, which means you don't need to commit months or years of your time to an asset that may or may not generate meaningful profit. So, short-term options trading means, generally speaking, less risks, less waiting time, and quicker gain opportunities. Sounds pretty great, right?

Fortunately, short-term trading is something both beginner and experienced options traders can take advantage of. The short-term trading strategies that you employ will of course depend upon your level and experience, and so, because this book is geared toward beginner options traders seeking to generate profit in just 48 hours, we'll be discussing several short-term trading strategies and suggestions in particular. These are foundational strategies that are easy to understand, and even easier to use. Sure, they're not the fanciest, nor are they the most impressive, but they won't require over excessive risks and won't put your financial status on the line.

Because this book revolves around helping you trade options successfully in just 48 hours, I'd recommend the following:

- Dedicate Day-1 of trading to understanding, practicing, and employing the first short-term strategy that we're going to discuss shortly—married put.

- Dedicate Day-2 of trading to understanding, practicing, and utilizing the second short-term strategy that we're going to discuss after married put—straddling. Married Put

Married puts are one of the basic, but surprisingly helpful, short-term trading strategies currently available to both new and experienced traders. Essentially, a married put, sometimes called a protective put, is when an investor buys shares of a stock, while simultaneously buying put options for those same purchased stocks. To break this concept down even further, consider this:

- John the options trader invests in stock A, B, and C.

- When he invests in stock A, B, and C, he also purchases put options for stock A, B, and C.

At this point you should understand why the married put strategy is an excellent choice—it's clear, simple, and reliable protection for your investments. But here's the best part: married puts, technically, create unlimited profit generation potential, and eliminate potential loss caused from downwards stock growth.

Straddling

The short-term options trading strategy of straddling can be, for some, a bit more complicated than married put. This isn't to say, however, that it's not an equally reliable and successful strategy for beginner traders to employ. With the straddling technique, investors will buy both a put and call option for the same stock, with the same strike price, and with the same expiration date.

Now, to fully understand how this strategy works, you'll need to be familiar with:

1. Put options

2. Call options

3. Strike price

Chapter 1's discussion about options types will help clarify any questions you have regarding what put and call options are. However, we haven't yet introduced what a strike price is in the world of options trading, so that's what we'll do now before moving on with our discussion about the straddling strategy. With that being said:

Strike price: the price at which the holder of a put or call option can buy or sell an asset; commonly referred to as an exercise price.

Example: Company XYZ's stock ABC is currently trading at $100. The stock shows promise (and constant upwards movement in market value), so you buy a call option with a strike price of $200. This means you maintain the right to purchase Company XYZ's stock ABC for $200, even after the stock's value increases to $350 just five days later. You maintain this right to buy at a pre-established price as long as you do so on or before the call option's expiration date.

If that makes sense, let's go ahead and move forward with our discussion of straddling. So, like we just learned a moment ago, the straddling strategy of options trading involves buying both a put and call option of a stock, with the same strike price and expiration date. Although it seems a bit complicated, all this really means is that you're protected on both sides—if the stock experiences a downward trend in stock value, you can sell at your pre-determined price, and if the stock experiences an upward trend in stock value, you can buy at your pre-determined price.

Straddling is a simple concept, but it tends to get a bit complicated when we merely use words to explain it. So, let's throw some actual numbers out there to help the more visual or math-orientated learners. Here's a scenario that involves the short-term strategy of straddling.

1.) Jane the options trader researches and discovers that stock CDF has experienced a steady upwards trend in price over the last 3 months. In April stock CDF was valued at $20, in May it was valued at $30, and in June it was valued at $40.

2.) Jane decides to approach this investment using the straddling strategy, so she buys both a put and call option for stock CDF in July when stock CDF has a $50 market price. Jane buys both call and put options with a September 1**st** expiration date and a $100 strike price.

Scenario #1:

- In August, stock CDF jumps in market value from $50 to $150. (Remember, Jane has both put and call options for this stock with strike prices of $100 on each).

- Seeing the profit she would generate if she exercised her call option, Jane does so. (Remember: with a call option, Jane has the right to buy an asset at the strike price agreed upon beforehand).

- Jane, using her call option, buys stock CDF (which has a market value of $150), with her strike price of $100. In the process, Jane generates a $50 profit, and exits her position.

Scenario #2:

- In August, stock CDF suddenly falls in market value from $50 to $30. (Again, remember that Jane has both put and call options for this stock with strike prices of $100 each).

- Jane notes the decline in market value, and decides she doesn't want to take any further risks, so she decides to exercise her put option. (Remember: with a put option, Jane has the right to sell an asset at the strike price agreed upon beforehand).

- Jane, using her put option, sells stock CDF (which has a current market value of $30), with her strike price of $100. In the process, Jane generates a $70 profit, and exits her position.

If you haven't yet gathered, the main idea behind straddling is this: a trader always has two options, and when one fails, the other protects against significant loss, and even generates profit. This double-layered protection is ideal for the beginner options trader.

Keep in mind, though, that strike prices require actual money. For simplicity's sake, this is something that I didn't include in the above scenarios, but it's important that you understand what's going on here with strike price. So, Jane bought a call and put option, each with a $100 strike price, right? Well, that was a $200 investment for Jane, since a strike price is essentially what you're paying the other person to "hold" an option opportunity for you. When we factor this into the scenarios, Jane isn't exactly securing a profit, is she? No, she's not. If we were to use this as a real-life scenario, Jane would be better off setting a lower strike price (maybe $40, for example), and waiting until the stock underwent a dramatic upward growth in price. I haven't done that here, though, because I wanted to show you plain and simple how straddling works. But now that you have that understanding for the strategy, I've been able to add one more layer—keeping in mind the initial investment you'll need to make in order to create a strike price.

Nonetheless, the two strategies of married put and straddling come highly recommended, not only by me, but by financial experts and investors who strive to help beginner options traders achieve financial success in the market arena. By understanding and employing these two crucial strategies (though not at the same time), beginner options traders put themselves in a good position.

However, there are further steps you can take to help you secure even greater success and help you generate even larger profit. The suggestions that you'll find below are excellent tips to keep in mind during your first 48 hours of trading and while you use short-term strategies, and both can be **combined** with one another as you use either the married put or straddling strategy.

Moving Averages

All a moving average indicates is the average price of a stock over a certain period of time. Moving averages can take the form of many timeframes, typically from 15 days to 200 days, and the most common timeframes are 20, 30, 50, and 100 days. Although it's quite simple, the moving average of a stock is something you'll want to keep track of quite closely because it provides a great indication of whether a stock is moving in an upwards or downwards trend. (This will help you determine, if you're using the straddling strategy, for example, whether you should exercise either your call or put option).

Moving averages are very easy to get your hands on. You can either 1.) keep track of a stock's market value on your own, and calculate its weekly or monthly moving average on your own as well, or 2.) Refer to stock charts and graphs, which are readily available, and always at your fingertips if you've downloaded a financial app such as:

- ChartIQ Pro

- StockSpy

- Daily Stocks

- WikiInvest Portfolio

If you do decide to keep track of moving averages, whether on your own or using financial tools, keep in mind that moving averages not only indicate when to invest, but when to exit as well. More experienced traders might tell you it's sometimes worth your time to stick around and see what happens if a stock's moving average begins to flatten or decline, though I don't recommend doing so, at least during your first 48 hours of trading when you're just starting out. Exiting an investment is always the safest route to take when stock values flatten or become static. Yes, you might lose out on profitable opportunities if the stock experiences a spike after you've exited, but you're also not taking the risk of losing money if the stock acts in the opposite way and experiences a sudden downwards spike in price.

Cycles and Patterns

If you know anything about the general stock market, it's that it's a highly volatile and unpredictable environment. I mean, it can be genuinely cruel...brutal...harsh. Use whatever word you'd like, but it is. At the same time, however, stocks usually fall under certain patterns and cycles that, when we pay close attention, we can take note of and use to our advantage. When we realize these patterns and cycles, especially those pertaining to our specific stock or future investment opportunity, we can make educated decisions about a stock's future movements, thereby giving us an upper hand in the cruel environment the stock market offers to its participants.

Research is, of course, a huge factor in discovering what these patterns and cycles are. I can't tell you what each and every stock's weekly, monthly, and yearly pattern and/or cycle is, of course, but what I can do is fill you in on a little secret: between November and April, stocks generally experience "gains" and upward trends (small or large), and between May and October, stocks typically undergo declines in price or experience static (unmoving) market statuses.

Again, financial tools and resources, like the apps I listed above, will help you research, learn about, and understand the particular cycles and patterns associated with your stock. I can't stress enough just how important research is during this entire process, even before your first 48 hours in the options trading market begins. Really, it's very crucial to your success, perhaps even more so than the short-term strategies and suggestions we've discussed in this chapter. Really, I mean that.

Chapter 6: Options Trading in the Forex Market

The foreign exchange currency market, or forex as it is typically called, is, without a doubt, the most lucrative investment market in the world. Each day it trades more than 4 trillion dollars which is approximately 10 times as much as the New York Stock Exchange. Despite this massive amount of trading, it was difficult for individual traders to take advantage of the market due to the technological limitations of the time. This is no longer the case; however, as the internet has given rise to numerous forex trading platforms which means that now forex trading is open to everyone.

Unlike many other types of markets, the forex market is purely speculative which means that nothing is actually changing hands when you place a forex trade. Rather, the forex market essentially only exists on various servers and databases worldwide with information coming in from countries all over the world causing these numbers to move in one direction or another. Each transaction is then tracked with any potential losses or a gain expressed in the primary currency of the country the database that is accessing the information is located in.

While this might seem like an odd system, it makes sense when you realize that the only reason the forex market exists is that major corporations and countries needed a way to convert currencies from one type to the other without going through a lot of cumbersome steps to do so. These major players tend to move amounts of currency that are vast enough to affect the actual value of the currencies being traded which is where the speculative portion of the equation comes into play.

Currently, only about 20 percent of the activity related to the forex market comes from these major players with the rest instead of coming from investors who are looking to make money based on the way the various currencies are reacting to the current market. A majority of these traders are professionals who work for financial institutions or hedge funds though more and more freelance traders are jumping on the forex bandwagon every day.

Forex basics: The most important thing to keep in mind when it comes to forex trading is that forex trades always consist of a pair of currency rather than a single asset like you would see in the stock or options market. What this means is that for every trade a forex trader is buying one currency and selling another. Currency is typically traded in 3 differing quantities, known as lots. A micro lot is 1,000 currency units, a mini lot is 10,000 units and a standard lot is 100,000 units.

The smallest amount that a given currency can move is one percent of its current total which is referred to as a pip. When you are first starting out with forex trading then it is recommended that you trade in micro lots as a single pip there is only work 10 cents of the currency in question. This means you will have less at stake during the early days when you are still finding your footing and you may often find yourself fighting against a market that has turned against you in unexpected ways. If you instead start with mini lots then with each pip of movement you are risking $10. To put this into perspective, the market frequently moves 100 pips or more in an average trading session.

While the forex market has several unique features that set it apart from other equities markets, it is the same in the ways that matter the most. Specifically, it is still driven by the core concept of supply and demand. As such, if a certain currency is experiencing high demand, then the value of that currency will increase accordingly until it reaches a point of oversaturation whereupon it will start to move back in the other direction. This means that as a forex trader you are going to need to be aware of when a given currency is going to increase in demand so that you can buy into it at the lowest price possible and thus reap the greatest rewards. This means you will always need to be aware of key interest rate movements, economic predications, and geopolitical strife.

Another important fact to keep in mind is that from Monday morning to Friday evening, the forex market never closes. Despite this fact, currency pairs are typically only traded during the times of day when the country whose currency it is are most active. Each trading day is generally broken into 3 chunks, Europe, US and Asia with the related currency pairs being traded during those periods.

This is the case because the currency pairs of those regions are always going to be more valuable during the periods of prime activity for the region in question. As an example, if you were thinking about trading a pair based around the US dollar and the Japanese yen then you would find that pair to be most profitable during the US hours and again during the Asian hours.

While there is currency pairs for essentially every combination of currency imaginable, the majority of forex trading can be broken down into 18 primary pairs. These 18 pairs are, in turn, made up of just 8 currencies that you are going to need to be familiar with if you hope to find success in the forex market. These are AUD the Australian dollar, CAD the Canadian dollar, CHF the Swiss franc, EUR the euro, GBP the British pound, JPY the Japanese yen, NZD the New Zealand dollar and USD the US dollar. Knowing what currencies to focus on and which to ignore, at least up front, is crucial to making the early days of forex trading as manageable as possible. There will be plenty of time for exploring lesser used currencies later, once you are completely comfortable with the basics.

Short-term strategy: If you are interested in trading options in the forex market in the short term then it is important to keep in mind that your goal should always be to control the amount of risk you take on as much as possible. This will make it easier for you to deal in charts that tend to offer shorter time frames than many forex traders deal in. This doesn't mean that you are going to want to stick to the short-term charts exclusively, however, as this can cause your profits to be lower overall than they would otherwise be.

To trade effectively in the short-term, the first thing you are going to want to be on the lookout for is a pair of moving averages on the hourly charts. The trading platform that you use should be able to automatically generate what you are looking for based on the timeframe that you choose. After you have the indicators that you are looking for, you will then be able to more easily utilize them as a sort of guidepost that will make it easier to determine how the market is moving in the timeframe in question so that you will be able to look before you leap as it were. If the resulting short moving average is less than the larger moving average then you will want to take a long position, otherwise, you will want to take a short position instead.

Once you have determined the trend that you are looking for, the next thing you will need to do is to look at the entries that are going to match the direction of the trend you are following. The goal here should be to successfully locate the momentum that you saw on the longer chart in either the 15-minute or 5-minute chart that you will actually want to do work in.

When putting this strategy to use, it is crucial that you keep in mind that it will not always be the right time to buy in. Instead, you are going to need to be patient and wait for a position that is profitable to open up and the best way to do so is to look for the exponential moving average. When seeking out the exponential moving average you are going to want to start by finding a trigger known as the 8-period exponential on the 5-minute chart which should be available from your trading platform. When this exponential starts to move in the direction of the trend you are following then you will know that it is a good time to go ahead and buy in.

While this strategy requires a good deal of micromanaging in order to be successful, it is also beneficial in several ways. The first of which is that if you choose to wait until you see the right trigger then you know that other traders are already creating action around the currency pair in question which means you can be fairly certain that the trade will be profitable. Additionally, this is a great strategy to use for those who have a lower amount of starter capital as it will make it easier to jump in on a given currency pair before the momentum picks up steam and the bullish nature of the pair causes the price to raise to a less tantalizing point.

In addition to making it easy to buy cheap, those who use this strategy when it comes to selling currency pairs they currently own will be able to do so to maximize their profits as they will be able to get out of a given trade before the masses do so, thus ensuring a higher price when they sell. It is important to remember, however, that the price could instead experience a short-term retracement which means you need to be sure of what the signals are telling you before you make a move if you don't want to pay the price for jumping out early.

In order to ensure a level of maximum profit with this strategy, you are going to need to set your stop losses at such a point that they are just underneath the last high that the currency experienced. If you are investing in short positions then you will want to set your stop losses so they are just above the current low price point instead. This will ensure that you don't lose out if the trend loses momentum before it reaches the price you are hoping for. By doing so you ensure that the short-term strategy remains as versatile as possible.

This strategy is not without risks of its own, however, as the short-term charts are prone to changing dramatically with little or no advanced notice. This means that if you hope to profit when using this strategy, you are going to need to make sure that you have the ability to react quickly to unexpected changes. The best reaction most of the time is going to be waiting for the currency to settle down before setting a new stop loss based on the new landscape that is slightly in the money without getting greedy.

Fibonacci retracement: To use a Fibonacci retracement, the first thing you are going to want to look for is a market that is trending. The general idea here is to go long on a retracement, a temporary reversal of direction in the price of the currency, at a specific level when the market is positively trending and to go short on retracements when the market is trending in the other direction. To find a retracement level you are going to want to find moments when pricing indicators you are looking for reach high, or low, points that are higher, or lower, than the average high, or low, point.

To understand the Fibonacci ratios that are useful in forex, it is important to understand the basics behind the Fibonacci numbers which were discovered by the man whose name they bear; they start off as 0, 1, 2, 3, 5, 7, 13, 21, etc. Essentially, to find the next number in the sequence you simply add the previous 2 numbers in the sequence together. Now, if you measure the ratio of each number to the following number in the sequence you get the Fibonacci ratios that are used in forex. These start off as .236, .382, .5, .618 etc. While the exact reason that Fibonacci ratios apply to the forex market isn't completely clear, it is clear that they resonate throughout the world at large from the smallest instance in individual molecules of DNA to the grandest in the organization of the planets in the sky.

Luckily, when it comes to utilizing the Fibonacci ratio in your trades, you don't need to memorize these numbers as all forex trading platforms will have a tool that will do the calculations for you. This means that all you really need to do is to learn how, when and why to use them in a technical analysis sense. It is important to keep in mind that Fibonacci levels are going to act as resistance as well as support for the price in question. As the price increases, the Fibonacci levels will act as resistance and as the price decreases, they will act as support. Additionally, much like with regular support or resistance they can be broken.

Trades that are based around the Fibonacci retracement on the charts for timeframes less than 10 minutes. Fibonacci retracements can be used to determine reasonable reward/risk levels either by selling a credit spread to the level in question or through buying options that are already in the money that are likely to experience a bounce at these levels. It is generally going to be in your best interest to look for Fibonacci levels that are likely to overlap at multiple timeframes as well as corresponding to the most recent trend experienced by the underlying stock. If you are so inclined, you can also utilize candlestick price patterns as a means of confirming a buy at specific Fibonacci levels.

Alternately, you may find success with oversold or overbought indicators when it comes to range-bound or trendless stocks. You can then sell credit spreads or buy into options that are already in the money and near the current level of resistance and support with tight stops. It is important to keep in mind that a given stock might not move quickly enough to make these levels worthwhile so it is important to do your research ahead of time in order to have a reasonable expectation about the future movement.

Indicators that are used to signal lower than average volatility such as Bollinger bands are especially useful when it comes to place trades that you anticipate big moves from. Breakout indicators time, especially for the shorter charts, is also especially useful.

Using the Fibonacci sequence to perform a retracement gives you the ability to determine how much an asset moved at price initially. It uses multiple horizontal lines to point out resistance or support at 23.6, 38.2, 50, 61.8 or 100 percent. When used properly they make it easier to identify the spots transactions should be started, what prices to target and what stop losses to set.

This doesn't mean that you should apply the Fibonacci retracements blindly as doing so can lead to failure as easily as it can success. It is important to avoid choosing inconsistent reference points which can easily lead to mistakes as well as misanalysis, for example, mistaking the wick for the body of a candle. Retracements using the Fibonacci sequence should always be applied wick-to-wick which in turn leads to a clearly defined and actionable resistance level.

Likewise, it is important to always keep the big picture in mind and keep an eye on trends that are of the longer variety as well. Failing to keep a broad perspective in mind makes short-term trades more likely to fail as it makes it harder to project the correct momentum and direction any potential opportunities might be moving in. Keeping the larger trends in mind will help you pick more reliable trades while also preventing you from accidentally trading against a specific trend.

Don't forget, Fibonacci retracements are likely to indicate quality trades, but they will never be able to do so in a complete vacuum. It is best to start with a retracement and then apply other tools including stochastic oscillators or MACD. Moving ahead without confirmation will leave you with little except positive thoughts and wishes that the outcome goes the way you want. Remember, there is no one indicator that is strong enough to warrant moving forward on a trade without double checking the validity of the data.

The other limitation of a Fibonacci retracement is that it doesn't work reliably over shorter time frames as there is simply too much interference from standard market volatility which will result in false apparent levels of support as well as resistance. What's more, the addition of whipsaws and spikes can make it difficult to utilize stops effectively which can result in tight and narrow confluences.

Chapter 7: The Option Pricing Models

The option premium is the actual price paid by the option holder for his right to exercise the option before it expires. This amount is paid to the option writer or seller. On the other hand, the option's theoretical value is the estimated option value, which is computed through a price model. It is the current value of the option that includes all factors, which change during the life of the option.

An option trader can use different price models to compute for the theoretical value. These models have forecasted and fixed values. Each of the variables can fluctuate over the option's lifetime. A lot of investors and traders use the updated theoretical value to monitoring the fluctuating value and risk of the option. They don't have to compute it by themselves. A lot of trading platforms offer updated values. There are also different websites which offer theoretical value calculators.

The Black-Scholes Model

As a method for computing option premium, it was published in the Journal of Political Economy as a paper entitled "The Pricing of Options and Corporate Liabilities". Two years after Black passed away, Merton and Scholes received the Nobel Prize in Economics in 1997 for their work. The option pricing model is used to compute the theoretical price of European call and put options and ignores any dividends paid during the life of the option. However, it is currently being adapted to take into consideration the dividends by determining the value on the ex-dividend date of the underlying asset.

The Black-Scholes option pricing model assumes that the options are exercised only on the date of expiration and the underlying asset doesn't pay out dividends during the lifetime of the options. Furthermore, it assumes that the price movements of the market are unpredictable. No commissions are also taken into consideration. The Black-Scholes model also assumes that the underlying asset's volatility and the risk-free rate are constant and known. Lastly, the returns of the underlying asset follow a normal distribution.

The Black-Scholes option pricing model may be intimidating and complicated to a lot of investors. However, these investors and traders don't need to know how to compute by themselves because there are various option price calculators available online. In fact, even option trading platforms offer these calculators. An investor only needs to know 5 variables: the risk-free interest rate, the number of days before expiration, the price of the underlying asset, and the option strike price.

The Cox-Rubenstein Binomial Option Pricing Model

This pricing model is a variation of the Black-Scholes pricing model. Proposed by John Carrington Cox, Mark

Edward Rubenstein, and Stephen Ross in 1979, this model became popular because the lattice-based model is used in considering the price of the underlying asset over a period of time. This lattice-based model considers the expected changes in different factors over the life of the option. As such, it produces a more accurate estimate of the option price. The Cox-Rubenstein Binomial model is used for American options, which can be exercised anytime until they expire.

Using a risk-neutral valuation, the Cox-Ross-Rubenstein option pricing model assumes that everyone is indifferent to risk and that the world is risk neutral. As such, the possible returns are the same as the risk-free interest rate. The model further assumes that arbitrage isn't possible and that for each period the price of the underlying asset can never go in opposite directions at the same time. It uses an iterative structure which specifies the time nodes between the present and the date of option expiration. It offers a mathematical valuation which creates a binomial tree where all possible values at various nodes are represented.

This pricing model assumes that the price of the underlying asset can only go up or down until the option expires. The price valuation starts with every final node and iteration are performed from the expiration date backwards up to the valuation date. It involves 3 steps: creation of the binomial tree; calculation of the value of the option at every final node; and calculation of the option value at every preceding node. The Cox-Ross-Rubenstein model is less complicated. However, like the Black-Scholes model, users can avail of the different online calculators. Trading online platforms also offer tools to compute the price values.

The Put/Call Parity

In his "The Relation between Put and Call Prices" paper in 1969, Hans Stoll defined the interconnection between the European call and put options with the same strike price and expiration. The call option price is the put option's fair value at a particular strike price. This relation came to be because the options' combinations created positions which were similar to the underlying asset's position. For this to hold true, both underlying asset and option positions must have the same arbitrage or return opportunity. Investors and traders can profit from this arbitrage, without risk, up to the point when the parity returned. Arbitrage allows the investor to profit from the differences in price of one underlying asset in various markets. As in illustration, if the trader buys a share of stock for $45 from one market while he simultaneously sell the same stock in another market for $50. This synchronized transaction can allow him to generate a profit from the trade with little or no risk.

In order to replicate the long position of an underlying asset, an investor can have a short put option and a long call option simultaneously. On the other hand, a short position of the underlying asset can be replicated by have a long put option and a short call option simultaneously. If the parity doesn't exit, the investor can profit from the arbitrage opportunities. An option trader can test the European option pricing model through the put/call parity. If the prices of put and call options don't satisfy parity, it means that there is an arbitrage opportunity. As such, the pricing model must be rejected.

For a non-dividend paying underlying asset, the following formula can be used to determine the option price:

$$c = S + p - Xe - r(T - t)$$

$$p = c - S + Xe - r(T - t)$$

Where:

c = value of the call option

S = current price of the underlying asset

p = value of the put option

X = strike price

e = Euler's constant (2.71828)

r = risk-free interest rate; compounded continuously

T = option expiry date

t = current valuation date

There are a lot of trading platforms which offer this tool. Some of these providers also offer put/call parity visual representations.

Profit And Loss Diagrams

A risk graph or profit and loss diagram is a graphical representation of an option strategy's potential profit and loss at a given time. An option trader can use this diagram to determine how his strategy can perform over different prices so that he can understand possible outcomes. To create the diagram, the prices of the underlying asset are plotted along the horizontal axis while the potential profit and loss numbers are then plotted along the vertical axis. The profits are plotted above the breakeven point while the losses are found below it. The resulting line graph represents the possible profit and loss on the range of prices of the underlying asset.

The Greek Values

The Delta computes for the sensitivity of the option price to fluctuations in the price of the underlying asset. It is an important Greek value because it indicates how the price of the option will move in relation to the price change of the underlying asset. Its value can range from 0 to 1 for call options. For put options, the value can move from 0 to -1. The delta value can also be represented from 0 to 100 for call options and 0 to -100 for put options so that decimals won't be used. An out-of-the-money call option can have deltas nearing 0. An in-the-money call option can have deltas nearing 1.

The Vega is a measure of the sensitivity of the price of the option to volatility changes of the underlying asset. It represents the changes of the option price to a 1% volatility change of the underlying asset. If there's still more time before the option expires, an increase in the volatility of the asset can have a greater impact on the option price. If there is an increased volatility, it means that the underlying asset may experience extreme values. Any increase in the volatility will have a corresponding increase in the option price. On the other hand, any decrease in the volatility will have its corresponding decrease in the option value.

The Gamma measures delta sensitivity in relation to the price fluctuations of the underlying asset. It measures the change in delta in response to every change in price of the underlying asset. Because deltas change at various rates, gamma measures and analyzes delta. It is useful in the determination of the stability of the delta. If the gamma results to a high value, it means that the delta can vary dramatically in relation to a small price movement of the underlying asset. An at-the-money option will give a high gamma. A low gamma is a result of an out-of-the-money or in-the-money option. If there's still a lot of time before the option expires, the gamma is low because the option is less sensitive to the changes in the delta. However, as the expiration date draws near, the gamma goes higher because changes in the delta have more impact.

The theta is a measure of the option's time decay, which is a theoretical value that the option may lose daily as it nears its expiration date. An at-the-money option increases the theta value while an out-of-the-money or in-the-money option decreases it. Long call and put options have negative thetas while short call and put options have positive thetas. A zero theta can result if the value of the underlying asset isn't depreciated by time.

Chapter 8: Fundamental Analysis

While it should come as no surprise that you are going to need to gather as much data as possible in order to make the best trades, regardless of what market you are working in; it is important to keep in mind that if you don't use it in the right way then it is all for naught. There are two ways to get the most out of any of the data that you gather, the first is via technical analysis and the second is via fundamental analysis. As a general rule, you will likely find it helpful to start off with fundamental analysis before moving on to technical analysis as the need arises.

To understand the difference between the two you may find it helpful to think about technical analysis as analyzing charts while fundamental analysis looks at specific factors based on the underlying asset for the market that you are working in. The core tenant of fundamental analysis is that there are related details out there that can tell the whole story when it comes to the market in question while technical analysis believes that the only details that are required are those that relate to the price at the moment. As such, fundamental analysis is typically considered easier to master as it all relates to concepts less expressly related to understanding market movement exclusively. Meanwhile, technical analysis is typically faster because key fundamental analysis data often is only made publicly available on a strict, and limited, schedule, sometimes only a few times a year meaning the availability for updating specific data is rather limited.

Fundamental Analysis Rules

The best time to use fundamental analysis is when you are looking to gain a broad idea of the state of the market as it stands and how that relates to the state of things in the near future when it comes time to actually trading successfully. Regardless of what market you are considering, the end goals are the same, find the most effective trade for the time period that you are targeting.

Establish a baseline: In order to begin analyzing the fundamentals, the first thing that you will need to do is to create a baseline regarding the company's overall performance. In order to generate the most useful results possible, the first thing that you are going to need to do is to gather data both regarding the company in question as well as the related industry as a whole. When gathering macro data, it is important to keep in mind that no market is going to operate in a vacuum which means the reasons behind specific market movement can be much more far reaching than they first appear. Fundamental analysis works because of the stock market's propensity for patterns which means if you trace a specific market movement back to the source you will have a better idea of what to keep an eye on in the future.

Furthermore, all industries go through several different phases where their penny stocks are going to be worth more or less overall based on general popularity. If the industry is producing many popular penny stocks, then overall volatility will be down while at the same time liquidity will be at an overall high.

Consider worldwide issues: Once you have a general grasp on the current phase you are dealing with, the next thing you will want to consider is anything that is going on in the wider world that will after the type of businesses you tend to favor in your penny stocks. Not being prepared for major paradigm shifts, especially in penny stocks where new companies come and go so quickly, means that you can easily miss out on massive profits and should be avoided at all costs.

To ensure you are not blindsided by news you could have seen coming, it is important to look beyond the obvious issues that are consuming the 24-hour news cycle and dig deeper into the comings and goings of the nations that are going to most directly affect your particular subsection of penny stocks. One important worldwide phenomenon that you will want to pay specific attention to is anything in the realm of technology as major paradigm shifts like the adoption of the smartphone, or the current move towards electric cars can create serious paradigm shifts.

Put it all together: Once you have a clear idea of what the market should look like as well as what may be on the horizon, the next step is to put it all together to compare what has been and what might to what the current state of the market is. Not only will this give you a realistic idea of what other investors are going to do if certain events occur the way they have in the past, you will also be able to use these details in order to identify underlying assets that are currently on the cusp of generating the type of movement that you need if you want to utilize them via binary option trades.

The best time to get on board with a new underlying asset is when it is nearing the end of the post-bust period or the end of a post-boom period depending on if you are going to place a call or a put. In these scenarios, you are going to have the greatest access to the freedom of the market and thus have the access to the greatest overall allowable risk that you are going to find in any market. Remember, the amount of risk that you can successfully handle without an increase in the likelihood of failure is going to start decreasing as soon as the boom or bust phase begins in earnest so it is important to get in as quickly as possible if you hope to truly maximize your profits.

Understand the relative strength of any given trade: When an underlying asset is experiencing a boom phase, the strength of its related fundamentals is going to be what determines the way that other investors are going to act when it comes to binary options trading. Keeping this in mind it then stands to reason that the earlier a given underlying asset is in a particular boom phase, the stronger the market surrounding it is going to be. Remember, when it comes to fundamental analysis what an underlying asset looks like at the moment isn't nearly as important as what it is likely to look like in the future and the best way to determine those details is by keeping an eye on the past.

Quantitative Fundamental Analysis

The sheer volume of data and a large amount of varying numbers found in the average company's financial statements can easily be intimidating and bewildering for conscientious investors who are digging into them for the first time. Once you get the hang of them, however, you will quickly find that they are a goldmine of information when it comes to determining how likely a company is to continue producing reliable dividends in the future.

At their most basic, a company's financial statements disclose the information relating to its financial performance over a set period of time. Unlike with qualitative concepts, financial statements provide cold, hard facts about a company that is rarely open for interpretation.

Important statements

Balance sheet: A balance sheet shows a detailed record of all of a company's equity, liabilities and assets for a given period of time. A balance sheet shows a balance to the financial structure of a company by dividing the company's equity by the combination of shareholders and liabilities in order to determine its current assets.

In this case, assets represent the resources that the company is actively in control of at a specific point in time. It can include things like buildings, machinery, inventory, cash and more. It will also show the total value of any financing that has been used to generate those assets. Financing can come from either equity or liabilities. Liabilities include debt that must be paid back eventually while equity, in this case, measures the total amount of money that its owners have put into the business. This can include profits from previous years, which are known collectively as retained earnings.

Income statement: While the balance sheet can be thought of as a snapshot of the fundamental economic aspects of the company, an income statement takes a closer look at the performance of the company exclusively for a given timeframe. There is no limit to the length of time an income statement considers, which means you could see them generated month to month, or even day to day; however, the most common type used by public companies are either annual or quarterly. Income statements provide information on profit, expenses, and revenues that resulted from the business that took place over the specific period of time.

Cash flow statement: The cashflow statement frequently shows all of the cash outflow and inflow for the company over a given period of time. The cash flow statement often focuses on operating cash flow which is the cash that will be generated by day to day business operations. It will also include any cash that is available from investing which is often used as a means of investing in assets along with any cash that might have been generated by long-term asset sales or the sale of a secondary business that the company previously owned. Cash due to financing is another name for money that is paid off or received based on issuing or borrowing funds.

While accountants can manipulate earnings with ease, it is much more difficult to fake having access to cash in the bank where there is none that really exists. This is why many savvy investors consider the cash flow statement the most reliable way to measure a specific company's performance.

Finding the details: While tracking down all the disparate financial statements on the company's you are considering purchasing stock in can be cumbersome, the Securities and Exchange Commission (SEC) requires all publicly traded companies to submit regular filings outlining all of their financial activities including a variety of different financial statements. This also includes information such as managerial discussions, reports from auditors, deep dives into the operations and prospects of upcoming years and more.

These types of details can all be found in the 10-K filing that each company is required to file every year, along with the 10-Q filing that they must send out once per quarter. Both types of documents can be found online, both at the corporate website for the company as well as on the SEC website. As the version that hits the corporate site doesn't need to be complete, it is best to visit SEC.gov and get to know the Electronic Data Gathering, Analysis, and Retrieval system (EDGAR) which automates the process of indexing, validating, collecting, forward and accepting submissions. As this system was designed in the mid-90s, however, it is important to dedicate some time to learning the process as it is more cumbersome than 20 years of user interface advancements have to lead you to expect.

Qualitative Fundamental Analysis

Qualitative factors are generally less tangible and include things like its name recognition, the patents it holds and the quality of its board members. Qualitative factors to consider include:

Business model: The first thing that you are going to want to do when you catch wind of a company that might be worth following up on is to check out its business model which is more or less a generalization of how it makes its money. You can typically find these sorts of details on the company website or in its 10-K filing.

Competitive advantage: It is also important to consider the various competitive advantages that the company you have your eye on might have over its competition. Companies that are going to be successful in the long-term are always going to have an advantage over their competition in one of two ways. They can either have better operational effectiveness or improved strategic positioning. Operational effectiveness is the name given to doing the same things as the competition but in a more efficient and effective way. Strategic positioning occurs when a company gains an edge by doing things that nobody else is doing.

Changes to the company: In order to properly narrow down your search, you will typically find the most reliable results when it comes to companies that have recently seen major changes to their corporate structure as it is these types of changes that are likely to ultimately precede events that are more likely to see the company jump to the next level. The specifics of what happened in this instance are nearly as important as the fact that statistically speaking, 95 percent of companies that experience this type of growth started with a significant change to the status quo.

Chapter 9: Technical Indicators

Technical indicators come into play in options trading when you need to determine turning points for underlying stock and the trends that get them to this point. When used correctly, they can help to determine the optimal time to buy or sell and also predict movement cycles. In general, technical indicators are calculated based on the pricing pattern of the underlying stock. Relevant data includes highs and lows, opening price, volume and closing price. They typically take into account the data regarding a stock's price from the past few periods, based on the charts the person who is doing the analyzing prefers.

This information is then used to identify trends that show what has been happening regarding a specific stock and then using past information to determine likely results for the future. Technical indicators come in both leading and lagging varieties. Indicators that lag are based on data that already exists and make it easier to determine if a trend is in the process of forming or if the stock in question is simply trading within a range. The stronger the trend that the lagging indicator pinpoints the greater the chance it is going to continue into the future. They typically drop the ball when it comes to predicting potential pullbacks or rally points, however.

When it comes to leading indicators, they are mainly useful when you are looking to predict the point in the future where the price of a specific stock is going to crash or rally. More often than not, these are going to be momentum indicators which, as the name implies, gauge the strength of the movement the underlying stock is going to undertake. Leading indicators tend to come in handy when you need to determine if the price the stock in question has reached is untenable in the long run and, if so, when the slowdown of the current trend is likely to occur. Because both oversold and overbought stocks are guaranteed to experience a pullback, knowing when this move is going to occur will come in handy more likely than not.

Both types of indicators are equally useful at different times, and often in conjunction with one another as you will frequently need to know both what types of trends are forming and when they are ultimately going to peter out if you are going to want to utilize most strategies successfully. In general, you are going to want to stick to a minimum of 3 indicators at all times.

Moving average convergence divergence indicator: The moving average convergence divergence (MACD) indicator is a type of oscillating indicator that generally moves between the centerline and zero. If the MACD value is high, then this indicates the related stock is close to being overbought, and if the value is low then the stock is in danger of being oversold.

MACD charts are generally based on a combination of multiple exponential moving averages (EMAs). These averages can be based on any time frame, though the most common is the 12-26-9 chart. This chart is typically broken into multiple parts, the first of which is the 26-day and 12-day chart. Using an EMA that is slower or fast allows you to more accurately gauge the current momentum level for the trend you are currently keeping an eye on.

If the 12-day EMA, the fast of the pair, ends up being above the 26-day EMA then you can safely assume that the underlying stock is in an uptrend while the reverse will also be the case. If the 12-day EMA increases at a rate that is greater than the 26-day EMA, then the uptrend is generally going to be even more pronounced. IF the 12-day EMA starts to move closer to the 26-day, then you can accurately assume that it is slowing down which means the momentum of the trade is going to fade. This, in turn, means you should expect the uptrend to end shortly.

The MACD puts these EMAs to use by considering the difference between them and then plotting it out. If the 26-day and the 12-day end up being the same, then the MACD will equal out to 0. If the 12-day ends up at a higher point than the 26-day, then the MACD will end up being positive. Otherwise, it will be negative. The larger the difference between them, the further the MACD line will fall from zero if the result is negative or from the center line if the result is positive.

By itself, this line does not provide any information that you would not be able to find from a simple moving average. However, it becomes much more useful once the 9-day EMA is taken into account as well. The 9-day EMA is different from the other 2 in that it shows the trend of the MACD line rather than the stock price. This means the 9-day EMA smooth's out the movement of the MACD line to make its results more manageable.

In addition to the 9-day EMA, you are also going to want to look at the MACD histogram which looks at the difference between it and the base MACD line. When the MACD line crosses above the 9-day EMA, the MACD histogram will typically cross above 0 and thus indicate a bullish signal. If it crosses on the other side of 0, then you can take that to indicate a trend that will turn bearish if it has not already. When put to a chart, the histogram will form in a series of peak that descends if the underlying stock is experiencing negative divergence and will generate a series of ascending peaks if it is experiencing positive divergence.

If the result generates a trend indicating negative divergence then you can feel relatively certain that the current positive trend is going to hit a level of resistance that it will not be able to overcome and, thus, reverse sooner than later. This can happen even if the pattern of the underlying stock has not started to run out of momentum quite yet. The same can be said about positive divergence and a negative trend. Remember the fact that these signals can become muddied if the price trades at or near the maximum range for a prolonged period. This means for the best results you are always going to want to use multiple indicators at once to prevent yourself from giving in to false signals.

Average directional index: The average directional index can be thought of as a guidepost that confirms the signals that other technical indicators bring to light. After a trend has been identified successfully, the average directional index can then more easily determine its strength compared to the other trends that are currently taking place. The average directional index is a combination of directional indicators that are both negative and positive and thus can more easily track trends regardless of their direction. They are then unified in a way that determines the overall strength of the trend.

As an oscillating indicator, the average directional index ranges between 100 and 0. The low end indicates that the trend is essentially flat and without volatility while the high end indicates that the stock is virtually moving straight up and down very quickly. This indicator is only useful when it comes to measuring the overall strength of the trend, not which direction it is moving in or is likely to move in anytime soon.

As a general rule, it is rare to see an average directional index value above 60. This is because trends with that much strength are only likely to appear in periods of deep recession or extremely long bullish market runs. What this means is that a value of anything greater than 40 can be considered a vibrant trend and anything lower than 20 indicates an underlying stock within a trading range.

When watching for average directional index signals, if a trend moves from above 40 to below it, then you can assume the current trend is slowing which means it may be time to mix up your current trading strategy or close out any existing positions. However, if you see a trend start at less than 20 and then increase to a point near 40 then you will know that a neutral market is starting to pick up steam and a major trend is likely going to be formed.

It is also important to always keep in mind the point where the negative directional index and the positive directional index cross. If the negative directional index is crossed by the positive in an upward direction, then you can assume the market is feeling bullish. If things happen the other way, then you can expect bearish trends instead.

Relative strength index: The relative strength index (RSI) is another type of momentum indicator that compares the relative magnitude of recent losses when compared to recent gains as a means of determining if a given stock is oversold or overbought. This, in turn, allows it to generate vital indications about the correlating reversals or corrections that are forthcoming, making price movements in the short-term clearer. RSI is most effective when used to measure individual stocks as opposed to indexes because it is more likely the individuals will experience either condition.

RSI values range from 0 to 100. Any value above 70 shows the stock is overbought and anything under 30 shows it is undersold. In general, options that are on high beta stocks with high liquidity are going to provide the best RSI results.

Some traders find that the RSI provides the most effective information when it is compared to crossovers with the short-term moving average. With the help of a 25-day and a 10-day moving average, you will likely be able to easily discern crossovers that show that a direction shift will occur in periods where the RSI is either in the range of 80 and 20 or 70 and 30. Regardless of what it shows, the RSI is always going to indicate a period of reversal, regardless of the precise direction.

The concept known as failure swings can make it easier for investors to take full advantage of the information shown through an RSI. Remember that just because the RSI shows either something in the range of 30 or 70, does not mean that the reversal is going to happen right away. Rather, positions can remain in overbought or oversold positions for an extended period. When the RSI extends to these levels, you are going to want to start watching the volume indicators to make it clear when traders start taking profits at the top or building up at the bottom. To make the most of this tool, it may be helpful to study old charts as a means of determining the types of price action you are likely to see at the opposite ends of an RSI, so you know what to expect.

Bollinger Bands: The importance of volatility when it comes to correctly valuing an option is well known. This is why Bollinger bands are as useful as they make it easy to grasp this facet of a particular stock, in turn, making it easier to identify lower and upper ranges. They work by generating bands based on the way the stock price has recently been moving. Bollinger bands tend to provide 2 types of indications:

- The bands tend to contract and expand depending on how volatility decreases or increases based on the way the price has been moving recently. If the bands expand then volatility is increasing, if they contract then volatility is decreasing. With this in mind, you can feel safer taking on reversal based option positions.

- The range of the current band can also be compared to the current market price as a means of determining any potential breakout patterns. If the breakout occurs at the top of the band, then you know the market has been overbought which means it is time to buy puts or short existing calls. If the breakout occurs at the bottom of the lower band, then you know the market is oversold which means it is time to buy short puts or calls that come with lower overall volatility.

- Either way, it is important to take care to assure the current volatility as shorting options if volatility is high can be beneficial. It can lead to higher premiums if volatility is high and cheaper options if volatility is low. The best value for a Bollinger band is up to the trader. However, the most commonly used value is 2 for the standard deviation of the top and bottom bands and 12 for the simple moving average.

The squeeze is the core concept of Bollinger bands as when the bands come close together they constrict the moving average and squeeze it tight, hence the name. A squeeze indicates that the volatility is going to be low for a time while the future likelihood is going to be increased, as will the number of potentially profitable opportunities to trade. On the other hand, the wider the bands end up being, the greater the likelihood of decreased volatility and the higher the likelihood that it is time to exit the trade. Always note that these two conditions are not trading signals in the traditional sense. The bands themselves give no true indication of what direction the price is likely to move in or when the potential change will take place.

Overall, Bollinger bands are not designed to be used in a vacuum. Rather, they are better served as an additional indicator which can then provide traders with additional information when it comes to the volatility of price. Ideally, you will want to use them with at least 2 other indicators that are non-correlated and also provide market signals that are more direct. Using Bollinger bands under these circumstances will help you to discover opportunities that you may have otherwise missed with an overall higher degree of success.

Intraday Momentum Index: If you tend to trade options more frequently than the average trader you are going to want to pay attention to the intraday momentum index (IMI) as it is a useful indicator when it comes to intraday trades. It utilizes candlesticks along with an RSI to create a useful intraday trading range by showing off oversold and overbought markets. Take into account how trendy these price moves are as if there is a visible, strong trend then the indicator might give off a false positive and read it as an oversold or overbought opportunity.

If you are aware of these trends, and also make use of the IMI, then you will have the ability to spot these types of incidents sooner than you otherwise would, making it possible to get into an early long position while the market is still on the uptrend or get into a short position if it is in a downtrend. You can determine the IMI with the following calculation.

1. **If Close > Open: Gains = Gain (n-1) + (Close - Open); Losses = 0**

2. **If Close < Open: Losses = Loss (n-1) + (Open - Close); Gains = 0**

3. **Add Gains and Losses for past n chosen periods**

4. **IMI = 100 x (Gains / (Gains + Losses))**

When combined with the possibility of leverage, the IMI can be a profitable technical indicator to use while you are trading options. The formula is also flexible in that each trader can use the n value that suits them best. Commonly used values include 70 or above for markets that are overbought and 30 or less for markets that are oversold.

Money Flow Index: If you are looking for a type of technical indicator to use as a complement to the RSI, the money flow index is a reliable choice. It combines volume and price data as a means of identifying price trends in a given stock. It is also known sometimes called the volume-weighted RSI. As volume is taken into consideration, this indicator can generate useful inputs regarding the amount of capital is moving into and out of the chosen stock over a set period of time. The most commonly used time frame is 14 days.

Put call ratio indicator: The put call ratio indicator (PCR) is useful when you need to determine the volume of call or put options that a given stock has attached to it. Rather than dealing in absolute value, the PCR indicates when the market's sentiment is changing. The greater the change in its value, the greater the change in the market as a whole. If the value drops, then this indicates a bullish trend which means more calls are being used. Likewise, a value that increases in value is going to show a trend towards bearishness and more puts overall.

As it is dependent on data regarding volume, the MFI indicator is especially useful for options trading based on stocks as opposed to indices. It is also known to see better results for longer forms of options trading than with intraday trading. In general, you will want to look for scenarios where the MFI indicator moves away from the stock price as this is generally a leading indicator that signals a trend reversal is coming. The best values to base your predictions on are going to be 20 for oversold and 80 for overbought.

There are two primary types of financial instruments, these include the primary securities and instruments as well as other instruments whose value is wholly derived based on their relationship to the primary instruments. When it comes to options, those underlying assets are securities which are what this indicator is looking at.

Chapter 10: Open Interests in Options Trading

Open interest reflects the strength of the market. It denotes the number of people interested in a particular trade. This is a very important number. Suppose a stock has been rising continuously but there are no open interests in that stock; it may mean that people are losing interest in that stock. You might face a problem with that stock as nothing can keep moving indefinitely without the active participation of the market.

Open interests provide a strong footing to any stock. It doesn't matter whether the stock is falling or rising, a large number of people interested in that stock will keep it alive and kicking in the market.

We can consider 4 scenarios to understand open interests

1. The prices of a particular trade are rising steadily. People are showing interest in that trade. This means the market is strong.

2. If the prices of a particular trade are falling continuously but people are still showing interest in it then it is a bad sign for the market. This will weaken the market and the prices will continue to fall.

3. If the prices of a trade are rising but people are not showing interest in that trade then it shows that the market has started weakening. This is a red flag.

4. If the prices of a particular trade start falling but there is a lack of open interest in that stock then this means the market is strengthening. People are more inclined towards buying than shorting the trades. It is a positive sign.

A good understanding of the open interests in the market will help you in speculating the trend of the market. It is an important factor and will help you in navigating the market safely.

You must understand that your guess cannot be much better than the guess of hundreds of others who are managing this market. The other thing is that the market runs on the sentiments, it doesn't really run on logic. If a thousand people are thinking something will make money then, believe me, it is already making money.

To take advantage and make money in the opposite market then either you have to be a genius or have some really good backing with a plan.

If you don't have any of these then it is safe to see the mood of the market and act accordingly.

Open interests give power to any stock. They keep the trades alive. Transactions keep ticking.

However, there is also another viewpoint on open interests. Some experts believe that open interests reflect the confidence of the option sellers. If there is any particular option trade that has a great number of open interests, then it wouldn't be hidden from the eyes of the option sellers. Selling a call option is a risk the seller takes. But it is not a blind risk. It is an informed risk. There are several calculations behind it. The seller knows with great accuracy that those levels wouldn't be tested. Otherwise, the losses would become unmanageable. It can happen once in a while, but the same thing occurring repeatedly can ruin any option seller. So, just following the open interests blindly can be very misleading.

Open interests reflect the mood of the market. They show that a stock is being actively traded on the stock exchange.

They also show the confidence of the buyers and the sellers on the stock.

Making the final deductions based on these facts will always be your prerogative.

Chapter 11: Ensuring the Benefits Outweigh the Risks

If you've been thinking about investing, have done some preliminary research, or have even had casual conversations with friends and family about investing opportunities, then I'm sure you've stumbled upon the popular topic regarding the benefits and risks of investing and, to be more specific, options trading. I know many of you are probably nodding in agreement (and perhaps experiencing a profound sense of boredom as I bring forth this topic), so you'll be happy to know that I won't be spending too much time on this topic.

If you've had the (fortunate or unfortunate, depends on your take) pleasure of **not** receiving an earful about the benefits and risks of options trading, then you'll find this chapter and the conversation in it to be of some importance.

Benefits

Rather than construct long-winded paragraphs that elaborate on the benefits of options trading, I've decided to forego the long discussion and, instead, include a simple but hopefully comprehensive list that advises readers about the many spectacular benefits they stand to gain by pursuing options. Keep in mind, though, that all of the following benefits won't come immediately, and for some traders, may never come, even. The benefits you receive from options trading depend upon your approach, your experience, your patience, and your dedication, so it's a nearly impossible task to predict which ones will grace your presence. But because you're a beginner trader, simply becoming familiar with the possible benefits of options trading is enough, at least in regards to your initial 48 hours of trading. (Because let's face it, you probably won't experience many of these benefits within your first 48 hours of trading. Many will come for sure, just not so soon).

Here's the list of options trading benefits that you can peruse on your own time:

- Call and put options, along with strike prices and premiums, allow traders not only to take calculated risks, but to have an idea of worst case scenario situations at all times. This lets you **plan ahead,** to gather some sort of idea for what to expect, and to prepare yourself for whatever situation you're confronted with.

- Options have "leverage," which means buying options can help an investor earn more per dollar than buying equity on a stock.

- Risk is significantly reduced with options— any potential for monetary loss is limited to the premium/strike price, so you won't be entirely affected if assets experience a dramatic loss in market value.

- Beginner options trading strategies are easy to learn and easy to understand, which means even beginner options traders can find relatively immediate and meaningful success when they begin trading.

- Option trading is highly flexible, especially when you start trading with different options forms—you can customize options contracts, select strike prices, and even decide expiration dates and cycles for investments.

- There are an array of financial resources, materials, tools, and mobile applications readily available at your fingertips, for little to no cost. In addition, there are a series of high-quality, local brokers and brokerages across the country that are happy to assist, advice, consult, and work for you. (Plus, you have the option to decide whether an online brokerage or human broker is the right financial advisor or tool for your personal financial situation).

Maximizing Your Advantages

We often talk about the benefits and advantages associated with options trading, but then the discussion stops there. There's rarely ever a continued conversation about how we can further branch off from those benefits or maximize our advantages. To help with this oversight, I've included the following section. It's brief, but it'll give the beginner options trader some sort of idea of what you can do within those first 48 hours in order to maximize any of the benefits or advantages you might be receiving from trading options.

- Hire a broker. Think of it this way: an individual trader gets his or her own particular set of benefits and advantages when they trade options, but when you hire a broker or brokerage to work on your "team," you get another whole set of benefits and advantages. Brokers open new doors, so use them to maximize benefits and gain new advantages.

- Utilize sell stops and buy stops. These are automatic actions that your broker or brokerage can handle for you. Sell stops are selling orders that you establish with your broker before pursuing an option or trade. You determine a pre-established price with your broker that indicates when your broker should sell an option. Buy stops work in the opposite manner; they are buy orders. These orders indicate to your broker when he or she should buy an option or stock, once it reaches a price you've previously agreed upon.

- Draft and stick to carefully outlined financial plans to ensure you don't stray in unwanted or unconducive directions. Determining beforehand what risks you're willing to take, and what risks you're not willing to take is extremely helpful during those first 48 hours of trading (when you're still getting a feel for how the market works and moves and how you personally operate as a trader).

Disadvantages

Again, I won't bore you with elaborate explanations of the disadvantages of options trading. Instead, here's another helpful list that clearly outlines why traders might choose to shy away from potential options trading opportunities:

- Options are time-sensitive investments. Yes, you can pick and choose options based on expiration dates, but you'll always be confined to a certain expiration date where you must choose to act, or choose to exit.

- Successful options trading require your attention and time. Without it, you risk losing out on potential profit generating opportunities that come from buying or selling your call or put option at the right, most profitable time.

- Options are without a paper-trail. With stocks and bonds, for example, you'll receive some sort of paper certification regarding your investment. Options are "book-entry" investments, meaning you receive no paper certification that shows your claim to an option or your ownership of an option.

- You're working in the stock market, a highly volatile place where changes occur suddenly and dramatically. You'll need to be on constant alert, or at least hire a broker who will.

- You'll need to be in a somewhat stable financial situation before you can successfully trade. Establishing and frequently adding to some sort of "trading fund" before you begin your options trading endeavors will somewhat remedy an unstable financial situation, however.

Reducing Your Risks

Similar to what we discussed earlier in this chapter, our conversations about the risks and disadvantages of options trading usually, well, end there. We rarely talk about how we can troubleshoot arising problems, or even reduce the degree of financial risks we must take in the first place. Though by no means extensive, I've included a short (but hopefully helpful) preview of the ways in which we can work on doing this with the first 48 hours of trading.

- Trade with this approach in mind: focus your attention and effort toward avoiding risks, rather than securing potential rewards. If you're not convinced, think about this little statistic recorded from a 2013 U.S Trust survey: 60% of millionaire investors place more emphasis on avoiding unnecessary risks than securing potential capital gain.

- Diversify your account. This is essentially just a fancy word for "split up your money to make it safer." When you don't put all of your eggs in one basket, so to speak, you significantly (and technically eliminate) the risk of losing all of your money when one investment opportunity cracks or crumbles.

- Keep a broker or brokerage close by. Beginner traders can benefit greatly from having a highly-trained, experienced financial expert or professional just a phone call or drive away. When trades don't go your way, or you're simply not deriving the benefits you expected from trades, even within that initial 48 hour timeframe, a broker can assist and advise you on how to produce better results and generate more meaningful profit. Or, they can attempt to remedy current, negative financial situations or trades.

Chapter 12: Avoiding Common Mistakes

Options are very risky, full stop. There are a lot of places where things can go wrong, and what's more is that it's extremely easy for people newer to the industry to make really simple mistakes that only take a little knowledge and foresight to avoid. The point of this chapter is to analyze these mistakes that a huge number of beginners will make so that you can avoid making them yourself and, hopefully, be a better investor yourself.

Buying cheap call options

Buying calls is absolutely not bad in and of it. But buying cheap calls can be very dangerous, and this is for a multitude of reasons. But before we discuss why it's dangerous, we have to examine why people do this in the first place.

The main reason that people are duped into buying especially cheap call options that are way beyond any sort of reality is, first off, because they're cheap. The low-price tag may present itself as a sort of "gambling" rather than "investment", but even if you're gambling, it's not much of a gamble if there's over an eighty percent likelihood that you'll end up losing the bet.

The other reason that one may be a cheap call option is because it fits a paradigm that they're accustomed to. After all, when you buy a call option, you're just making the prediction that the stock will go up in price, right? And that's the notion that a lot of people make when they're selling **equities**. The whole "buy low, sell high" paradigm absolutely rules the sphere of equity trading. So this is a comfortable paradigm to transfer over to options trading. It doesn't feel too far off from what you know.

However, this is a terrible idea to transfer over, and I'll tell you why: when you buy cheap options, you are buying options which are cheap for a very specific reason. Remember how we talked about things that can affect options premiums? Well, that lesson should apply here. Low cost options contracts are low cost because they aren't expected to pay out well; they're low demand, so the broker doesn't have to ask much in order to make a decent amount off of it.

What's more is that when you buy options on a stock, as we've already discussed, you're already taking into account the timing of a stock hitting a high or a low. Its price will be affected by the likelihood of it going in a specific direction.

In other words, cheap call options are generally cheap because they aren't going to go anywhere, and you'd have to have a miracle and a half to not lose the entirety of your options premium that you paid down, let alone make a profit.

So what can you as a beginner do instead? You should build your equities portfolio and instead **write** calls on stocks that **you own**, rather than **holding** calls on stocks that **others** own. When you do so, what you're basically saying is that you'll sell the stock that you own at the strike price in the option. Since in calls, the price is generally higher than the **strike price**, the risk is minimal. You, as the writer, are simply saying to the holder "if the stock goes up to the strike price, I will sell it at that price, even if it is above the strike price." This means that regardless of what happens, you make a profit, it's just not **quite** as high as it would be otherwise.

This technique is called the "covered call". It's a great way to make a fair amount of early income, and it's relatively safe for you as the writer. The only way that this method could displace your capital is if the stock goes significantly down (more than normal market fluctuations) since the time that you'd invested in it. However, it does limit your ability to sell if your stock goes exponentially up, as it gives you an "earnings" ceiling. But regardless - though you may not become a multimillionaire off of one stock boom, you'll make a steady profit off of selling contracts to your investments.

Moreover, if the market doesn't really go anywhere and just stays flat, and your stock's market price never hits the strike price, you still obtain the premium from the contract buyer for selling him the option in the first place. Meanwhile, you maintain your stock, of course, to repeat the process once more once the expiry date has been reached on a given contract.

So this is a much safer way to get to know the options market as you're just starting out and make a steady amount of income rather than simply going gung-ho on certain out of the money calls. What's more is that instead of putting you in a position to take **risks**, you're putting yourself in a position to be the **risk which others take**. You are in a secure position; if the market stays flat, or goes down a bit; you collect a small premium and maintain your stock. If the market rises to the stock price, you still profit - though maybe not as much as you would have liked to - and can use the resultant capital in order to invest in another stock and repeat the process. The only risk you're undertaking in this scenario is the possibility that your invested capital is devalued. However, the chances of a major crash are much lower, and you still have a certain amount of steady income from the covered calls on the stock.

No plan

This is a critical killer. With anything, it's important to have a "way out" if things don't go your way, and be able to control your emotional reactions should things shift for the worse. However, it's of absolutely paramount importance in the trading game, in a manner which really can't be understated at all. Having a plan is important in every single trade that you'll ever make, and having a sort of "exit" plan is most definitely important, too.

So what do I mean by "have a plan"? It's simple. You need to have a plan in place that you can minimize losses if your trades go for the worse and maximize gains if they go for the better. And this doesn't necessarily mean forming some sort of bizarre clairvoyance for the market and knowing exactly what's going to happen.

Rather, it's about recognizing patterns and developing a finite way for you to react to these patterns. This is absolutely imperative, actually. If you don't do this, then you're going to find yourself taking massive losses waiting for an option to go in the money as you near your expiry date, or you're going to find your options taking turns for the worse because you wanted to wait around and see if a stock would continue to go up.

You need to set up a plan for yourself: what sort of gains will make you happy as a trader when you're on the upside? What is the worst you'll allow things to get on the downside before dodging out? Evaluate how trades have gone wrong before and specifically factor in for those. Do you have a habit of getting a bit greedy and losing good deals because a given stock did a 180 and ended up losing more than you would have gotten otherwise? Do you have a habit of holding onto stocks for too long when they're bad and losing more money than is necessary in the process? Identify those and specifically set up plans for those traits in particular.

Illiquidity

Liquidity essentially means the ease with which a person can buy or sell something without there being a significant change in the price of that thing. This means that there must always be a large amount of active traders within the market. In a mathematical sense, liquidity as a concept represents the likelihood that the following trade will be around the same price as the prior one, preferably with the two trades being of equal price.

Options markets are by their nature less liquid than stock markets are because stock markets operate on a simple notion of equity. You sell a share, you buy a share, that share represents the essential concept of a piece of something bigger, but there's little way to change that share. That share is that share, basically. Options markets, however, offer a variety of different contracts. On options markets, one may buy a long call option, a long put option, a short call option, a short put option, and any variation of options contracts therein. They can buy American style options or British style options. They generally have a lot more variance in both the mechanisms of trade as well as the things which are being traded themselves. Because of this, options markets **are** far less liquid than stock markets, because there's so much more variance for people to account for.

A company which trades constantly is unlikely to be a liquidity issue, regardless of whether you're operating on the stock market or the options market. However, if a company is smaller or has stock which trades far less frequently, then it's much more illiquid.

It follows that if a given stock should be illiquid, because of the different mechanisms at work then the options contracts available to that same company will be even more illiquid. This means that the bid and ask price for options become very artificially distant. This means that a lot of money would be spent in order just to establish a position. (Stock lingo for "buy it"; "clear your position" means to sell stock)

So what can you do to prevent this? The easiest way is to avoid trading illiquid options, simply put. Research every single investment you make very well, and be certain that the interest in the stock is incredibly high. Trading illiquid assets can be a massive setback and cost you far more than you'd make off of it, and it will save you a lot of stress too. There are a huge number of opportunities for good liquid options contracts that are readily available to you.

Trading options can be incredibly difficult. Here, I only put the three most egregious examples which came to mind, but all of them are extremely common and admittedly tempting mistakes that beginner traders will make in the world of options trading. It's important that if you want to grow as a trader, you recognize as many of **other** people's mistakes as you can. If you do so, you're making silently sure that you don't make those same mistakes yourself; in effect making you a far better trader than you would be otherwise.

Conclusion

The next step is to implement all of this. Learn, learn, learn, and at some point take the jump to invest and start learning by experience.

I feel like I need to reiterate this one last time for good measure: options trading is dangerous. It's not something that you can just passively be involved in, and honestly, it's not a good place for any beginning trader to get involved in. It takes a lot of extensive theory and knowledge about exactly the things you're working with, and you're going to find often that you'll be losing instead of gaining -- especially as a beginner trader.

What are the ways to circumvent this? Well, there isn't. The obvious route is to simply go with something more lucrative and less risky. For example, if you just invest in equities and indexes, you can expect something like a six percent growth rate. After all, the economy is growing constantly. Neoliberal economic policies only exacerbate this sense of growth such that if you can actually afford to make a reasonable investment into equities or indexes, you will almost certainly see a positive return on it, albeit a smaller one.

Some time ago, before I devoted myself to studying finances and learning how to be a good investor, driven mainly by an intense interest in the way that the markets ticked and worked and the way that wealth moved around in our economy, a friend shared with me some very pertinent advice: "you're better off investing in yourself than investing in stocks." Since then, that's somewhat resonated.

Investments are called investments for a reason: they're long-term investments intended to accrue a certain amount of revenue over time, and if the company in which you invested does well, you too will benefit from the resultant success of course. That's the nature of investments.

But it's also a very impersonal and unsure way to make money. If you're looking for a get rich quick scheme, this is not it. Investing has a whole lot of upsides and can be a lot of fun and an absolutely crazy ride. But that doesn't mean that it's intended to make you a ton of money. If you're looking for localized investment with high returns, there are better ways to do it, such as learning about making money by affiliate marketing or creating worthwhile content.

The long and short of it is that investing is intended for people who have extra money. It's not intended for people to make extra money. Some just happen to. Most, in fact, do, but it's very, very unlikely that you're going to be the next Warren Buffet because of investment, especially in options trading.

And that goes further to say that if this is really what you want to do, be prepared to lose some money in the process. Options trading are hard to get into as a beginner, and take a fair amount of capital to even get a decent start. However, if you decide that it's what you want to do, here's how I can sum up the path for you going forward.

The first thing is to only even consider doing options trading with your speculative capital. What speculative capital means is money that you can set aside and essentially afford to lose should things go awry. Never, ever invest money that you genuinely need. Before doing any sort of investiture, be certain that you have at least 3 months of emergency savings set up and that you can afford to lose every single cent that you're putting into it. There's not a successful trader that won't tell you this. This isn't to turn you away from investing; it's a very real way to make very real capital gains... if you know what you're doing. But every single worthwhile trader out there will tell you to prepare to lose. Don't ever do anything that puts you in a worse position than you started out in. Only ever invest capital that you do not need.

The second thing is to spend a fair amount of time doing research. Research is ultimately the name of the game in any sort of investing. A part of me feels like that goes without saying, but it should be driven home that it is absolutely the case. Research is the fundamental crux of every decision that happens in the marketplace. It's only by knowing about a company, about its founder and its board and about its upcoming products, by knowing its past history and its marketplace trends, by knowing the trends of the market in general, by knowing what things like beta bid/ask are and how they have an impact on the viability of an options trade, and by knowing in-depth a lot of key concepts on the marketplace that you can even think of becoming a renowned options trader.

The third thing is far less general - you're going to have a much easier time starting out as an options trader if you build a portfolio and then proceed to sell contracts on those options. It will give you a much kinder sandbox with a lot less shards of glass where you can learn the ins and outs of options trading while still being a safe distance away from any real economic harm. Every single new options trader should spend a lot of time doing covered calls until they feel as though they sufficiently know the market and what they're doing and how they have a hand in the market at large.

In the end, if you feel like trading, you absolutely should. I genuinely hope that I've given you enough foundational information such that you can make informed decisions about the things you'll be doing on the market. Options trading, as I said, can be very lucrative if you know what you're doing. My goal in writing this book was to help set you up to know what you're doing.

So if you've made it past all my warnings and second-guess and you've decided that you still definitely want to move forward on options trading, and then what are you waiting for? Go back to one of the brokers we discussed in chapter four and start an account. Does some research before you make a deposit so that you're sure this is the step you want to take, and once you're positive, take the steps you have to get into the game?

Options trading is endlessly fun and rewarding if you find yourself interested in these sort of things, and I can't help but feel like you'll very much enjoy your time spent doing it if you've made it this far into this book. So go for it!

TRADING OPTIONS

The ultimate guide in trading with profitable ideas and strategies for great passive income in generation by option trading

[Michael Swing]

Text Copyright © [Michael Swing]

Legal & Disclaimer

this book as and when needed. Where appropriate and/or necessary, you must consult a professional (including but not limited to your doctor, attorney, financial advisor or such other professional advisor) before using any of the suggested remedies, techniques, or information in this book.

Upon using the contents and information contained in this book, you agree to hold harmless the Author from and against any damages, costs, and expenses, including any legal fees potentially resulting from the application of any of the information provided by this book. This disclaimer applies to any loss, damages or injury caused by the use and application, whether directly or indirectly, of any advice or information presented, whether for breach of contract, tort, negligence, personal injury, criminal intent, or under any other cause of action.

You agree to accept all risks of using the information presented inside this book.

You agree that by continuing to read this book, where appropriate and/or necessary, you shall consult a professional (including but not limited to your doctor, attorney, or financial advisor or such other advisor as needed) before using any of the suggested remedies, techniques, or information in this book.

Introduction

The buying and selling of stocks originated from floor trading to phone transactions. However, neither of those methods are still popular today. Today, online trading (or E-trading) is the most common method for exchanging stocks. Fast computers and high-speed internet have opened the doors to this ease of access. These have increased the number of people who can use it. Unlike before, you do not have to be rich to enter the world of online trading. Even commoners can invest in stocks.

Online trading is very convenient. With just a few clicks, people can easily participate in buying and selling stock activities online. In addition, the process of registering is very easy. You only have to find an online platform or an online broker to be able to start. Here is a systematic guide on how to start online trading.

How Online Trading Works

First, you need to determine how long you will be trading. Do you prefer short-term or the long-term investments?

Long-term investments require knowledge on cash flow, earnings, book value, return on earnings, etc. These concepts are fundamentals when it comes to stock analysis. On the other hand, if you want to enter "swing trading" or short-term investment, you should also know the technicalities of stock trading. This information is essential in order to decrease the risk of losing.

Upon deciding on whether you prefer short term or long term investments, you then will need to follow the steps below.

1. Find an online broker.

2. Choose an account to register.

After you have registered, find an online platform where you can create transactions. A tip is to research before you invest. There are sites available where you can check the credibility of the platform. However, you can never tell how it works unless you really use it.

The next step is to place an order. Here is an example on how trading takes place in NASDAQ.

1. Place the order.

2. A database will receive the order.

3. The database looks for the best price among all the available markets.

4. After finding the perfect match, the parties will receive a confirmation.

5. Regulatory bodies will check the stock's performance.

6. Data is analyzed by NASQAD.

7. Last, after agreeing upon the terms and price, the buyer and the seller will receive a notification from the broker about signing the contract.

Usually, it takes one second to place an order and the whole transaction for about one minute. This is the reason why people are so engrossed with online trading. It is definitely fast and exciting.

Types of Online Trading

There are three types of online trading:

1. Day Trading

Based in its name, day traders only place their bets on intraday basis. They do not let it sit overnight because of the higher risk of losing. Aiming to earn quick profits, these traders observe the fluctuations throughout the day and grab the best deal they can get.

Sub-types:

- Momentum Trading

- Scalpers

2. Swing Trading

Day traders and swing traders are quite similar. The only difference is that, swing traders can hold their position in the stock market for more than one day. In addition, swing traders base their bets on predicting short-term fluctuations. The downside is there is a higher risk of losing in overnight trades.

3. Position Trading

This is the same as swing trading, but position traders can hold their bets from a day to several days or months depending on the movement of stocks. They will wait for a huge rise in stocks before they get it.

Online Trading to Gambling

Technology has been a great help for people who love to invest in stocks. With only few clicks, you will be able to conduct research about the company you want to invest in. Plus, you have a wide variety of options. You can think it over and get back to the trading platform when you are ready while monitoring the rise and fall of stocks is in real time.

Because it is more accessible, people are attracted to investing. This creates a more strong hold to trading - making it more possible for people to get addicted.

Online trading only becomes a form of gambling if people keep on investing on high risk bets.

Consistent failure means they are already addicted. They do not think before they act. They simply love the feeling they get from it - the excitement from the uncertainty. They do not research. They make decisions based on their gut feeling.

Why Does Online Trading Feel So Good?

Making money is very easy in online trading. You place your order in about a second and you can immediately reap what you have invested within minutes. It doesn't matter if sometimes, you lose. What is important is that, the more you keep playing, the higher your chances of winning.

That is the reason why many online traders became online gamblers. They keep investing and placing orders to earn a lot of money. The downside is some online traders keep sliding down the slope – frequently placing orders and eventually draining all their resources. These people become so obsessed that they forget how to weigh their options and make wise decisions. They have lost control of themselves.

Adverse effects may happen if they do not stop. They are not only putting their lives to waste but they are also affecting the lives of their family members and friends by always being unavailable and uncontrollable.

Reasons Why Online Trading is Addicting

How can online trading be addictive to people who are aware of the pros and cons of the situation? The answer is simple: they are addicted to the feeling they get from it. People who become addicted to online trading are those who find high-risk decisions exciting. But, that is not the sole reason. There are many other causes of addiction depending on the person's personality and the situation. Here are 5 major reasons why people get addicted to online trading.

1. Easy

In Chapter one, you learned that joining online trading is very easy. With a few clicks, you can create an account, register, fund your chosen account, and then place an order. The process can take place in less than an hour. Plus, the trading itself happens within a minute.

If a manager of a specific company works hard to be a billionaire, a wise online trader can also level with the manager's earnings by having a good strategy and waiting for the prices to rise.

2. Fast

Not only that the process is easy, but it can also raise your money quickly. By following the simple procedure, you can place an order and wait for it to profit. If after a minute the market went up, and you are satisfied with your profit, then you can sell it immediately.

3. Happiness

People tend to stick to the things that make them happy even if it's dragging them down. It is the excitement from the unknown and the risk from placing their investments without thinking it over that makes them stay.

4. Relieves Stress and other Unpleasant Emotions

If you are trading because you wanted to relieve yourself of stress, then it is a strong reason for you to stick to it. Since it is fun and exciting, it will definitely soothe you and divert your attention.

5. Diversion from a Problem

Finally, aside from relieving you of stress, it can be a good diversion from a problem. Placing bets and waiting for it to profit can occupy your mind and reject unwanted thoughts.

The Passionate Trader versus the Trading Addict

There are two kinds of traders: the Passionate and the Addict. Both are dedicated to online trading, but their purpose and decision making strategies are very different. A passionate trader can handle his or her trades well, calculate the risk and base his or her decision depending on the flow of the market. On the other hand, a trading addict bases his or her decisions on emotions. Addicts do not analyze the situation logically, rather they place an order on high risk companies because of the excitement they get from it.

At first look, they may not seem different at all, but as you thoroughly analyze them, you'll clearly see the pattern of their behavior.

Passionate Trader

A passionate trader takes his or her time to think about the decisions to be made. Every single detail counts so he or she is not careless in deciding. This trader is also called the wise trader – aware of the options and the pros and cons of the situation. The goal of a passionate trader is to make money with the optimum possibility wherein risks and losses are avoided.

Trading Addict

On the other hand, a trading addict is someone who places their stocks without analyzing the situation. If they feel like placing an order, buying and selling stocks, they will do it – without any hesitation. It is as if they are standing on a vast ground of sand. Nothing is permanent. If there is a sand storm, they'll be easily washed away by it without even noticing what happened. They are blinded by their purpose, which is to easily make money by taking high risk investments.

With these descriptions, you can't really tell whether a person is a passionate trader or a trading addict unless you closely observe how they trade. However, the trading addict creates a situation wherein everybody, including his or herself will soon be damaged.

At What Point Does Online Trading Become Addictive & Suck You In?

There is a very thin line between online traders and online gamblers. Most are trading to profit immediately without analyzing the market or the pros and cons of their decisions. They are not only negatively affecting themselves, but also affecting others as well. Sooner or later, they will reap what they have sown – an evil seed that will bear an evil fruit.

6 Adverse Effects of the Addiction to the Online Trader

Soon, the boomerang will definitely hit you. If you are gambling for profit and continuously betting the wrong way, then, you'll be surprised on how fast you'll be eaten by the quicksand you have created. The effects of addiction to an online trader are very adverse. You can't undo it. It will gradually pull you down.

1. Draining Finances

The most obvious effect is on the financial aspect. If you are an addict, you place bets without even thinking about the risks and it will most likely drain your resources. High risk investments have probabilities of less than 50%, meaning lesser chances of winning. This can result in continuous losing and you'll surely end up with an empty pocket.

2. Health Effects

Eye strain and back pain are two common problems of an online trader. Long hours of sitting in front of the computer will strain the eyes. It will also cause back pain because of long hours of sitting and waiting for the stock market to rise.

3. Sleep Deprivation

If you are addicted to trading, day traders as an exception, you will be a bit paranoid on how the market will fluctuate overnight so you keep thinking about it. You will not be able to sleep well. It may worry you and keep you awake overnight. This will leave you sleep deprived. Your immune system will also weaken because of the continuous lack of sleep.

4. Decreased Productivity

Addiction will also eat away all the time you have. In this case, you will not be able to do anything aside from trading. You don't want to miss a second without placing an investment. You keep track of what's happening every second. It occupies mind and your life.

5. Poor Work Performance

If you have a job, you'll definitely sacrifice it for online trading. You won't be able to give your one hundred percent to your work. Between office hours, you'll see yourself checking on the stock market. Trading would be the only thing that matters.

6. Isolation

Imagine this: if 24 hours a day, 7 days a week your main focus is trading, then you'll eventually become isolated from the people who care about you. You will not seek for any attention or security, for that matter, because the most important in the world is to trade and to win.

7. Detachment from the World

The end point of being an addict is the detachment from the reality. You'll be lost in the world of trading and it will be hard for you to come back.

3 Effects of the Addiction to the Friends and Family of the Online Trader

1. Time

Relationships with family and friends will soon wither and die because you lack time to hang out with them. You are so occupied that you focus all your energy in that sole activity – trading.

2. Attention

The family should come first no matter what. But if you are an addict, even talking to your spouse and your children would be a burden. You do not want to be disturbed by anyone when you are trading. Your attention is focused on whether you'll win or lose.

3. Financial Support

If you are really an addict to online trading all your resources will be drained. This will result to drainage of money to support the family. In some cases, an online trading addict will steal from the family's money and use it in trading. In the long run, the family will also suffer from poverty because of you.

Now, you need to know the signs of being addicted. The following is a quick list:

- You spend most of your time placing bets.

- You do not do anything productive.

- You cannot detach yourself from the computer screen. It is hard to distract you.

- You keep on placing bets without considering the consequences.

- You enjoy the feeling of placing high-risk bets.

- You bet because of impulse and gut feeling.

- You love uncertainty.

- You keep losing and still place more bets, not realizing how much you have lost.

If you suspect that you are already a trading addict, then, continue reading this book. The succeeding chapters will discuss different strategies to aid you in overcoming your addiction to online trading and how to get your life back immediately.

Chapter 1: What is finance marketing

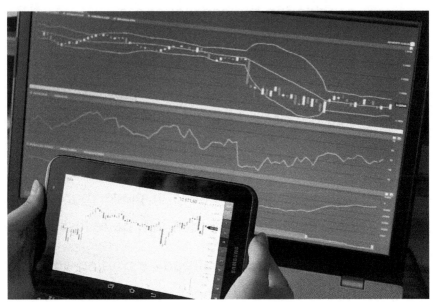

What Is An Option?

First, let's try to understand what options are if you are not yet familiar with them. You might already be using them now. Imagine that you're the head of a movie studio.

The stock market may seem like a scary world to people only taking their first steps in it, but there are actually a variety of securities investors that people have at their disposal. One such security, known as an "option," opens the door to a world of opportunities for investors.

'Options' actually refer to contracts between two parties (buyer and seller of financial instruments) giving the former party the rights to sell or acquire underlying assets. The options also contain details of price and validity of the particular assets being traded. In option trading activities, you can actually protect your financial position from decline by prompt adaptations to the changing market behavior. Since there are numerous factors that influence business transactions in the option market, success in this field comes with experience and knowledge.

Options are one more way of making your money work for you while protecting against undue risk. Options are derivatives; that is, the value of an option depends on the value of the financial instrument upon which it is based and, in the case of options, the behavior of the market while the option is in effect. The value of stocks and bonds is based on the firm or organization issuing the instrument.

For example, a stock issued by a company that is about to go bankrupt has little or no value, compared with the stock of a financially stable firm that is a leader in its industry. Similarly, a bond from a city that is thriving and has a good revenue base is more valuable and has lower risk than a bond from a city that is on the verge of bankruptcy.

A number of considerations have to be understood before partaking in this risky area, however. Option trading is not always based on stocks. An option is defined as a derivative financial instrument that involves a specific contract between two parties. Options involve future transactions. The option is itself is usually attached to an underlying financial asset. The option involves a future transaction affecting a specific asset with a set price, known as a strike, price. Whenever you see the word "future" in a transaction description, think of an option. An option can be exercised, or acted upon, when the strike price is satisfied.

Option prices are dictated in part by the difference between the strike price and value of the option's underlying asset. In addition, premiums are added to the option price to properly compensate the seller. Premiums are typically based on how much time is left before the expiry of the option, known as the expiration date. Any type of valuable asset can have an option created for it. An option transaction always involves a buyer and a seller, as with any contract. The option provides the buyer the mandate to purchase the instrument. The buyer is under no obligation to purchase the option. The option seller, however, incurs a legal obligation to fulfill their end of the transaction.

One party is usually well-capitalized, as in an investment bank. These options are not regulated. Terms are unrestricted and up to the individual parties to serve specific purposes. Common OTC options include swaps, currency cross rates and interest rate instruments.

Another type of trading option is listed on any number of options exchanges, generally known as futures and options exchanges. Hence, these options are known as listed options. Instead of private parties handling the details, trading houses handle the transactions. And, all options must be settled via the clearing house. The trading exchange uses its credit worthiness to guarantee that options are fulfilled. Examples of these options include standardized contracts involving bonds, stocks, any futures contract, stock market indexes and callable contracts.

Employee stock options are another form of options that, depending upon the terms, can be traded. These options are usually awarded by the firm as an incentive, or employee benefit. Usually firms owning the asset handle the options trading, with the approval of the employee involved. Four types of options trading exist. They are a long call, long put, short call and short put. All involve extensive details that depend on what the trader believes will happen to the stock price. For instance, a long call gives the trader the right to purchase the stock, known as a call option, when they believe the price is going up.

Option trading has more risks if you do not understand what you are doing, since they are so speculative in nature. All facets of an option change throughout the exchange day. A premium in place when you purchase an option may change by the time you sell the option, for instance. Or, the underlying financial asset may change for any number of reasons. Making money from option trading is not easy but with the right training and the right knowledge, option trading can be highly profitable with a high winning probability ratio.

As previously stated, an option is a right, but not an obligation. Of course, if you let the option's expiration date pass by, the option will become unprofitable-and you will thus lose 100% of your investment. Keep in mind, too, that an option is merely a contract that deals with an underlying asset. In our imaginary scenario, the piece of art was the underlying asset. An option is also called a "derivative," because it derives its value from something else (i.e. the piece of art).

Let's look at another example. A sales person calls you to set up a meeting with you. You can tell from the excitement in his voice that he thinks he is onto something big. Playing it cool, you tell him that you are busy. You request to make up for the meeting some time the week that follows.

As the person in charge of a movie workshop, it looks like you have listened to a million of these pitches. Some have been brilliant, while others ridiculous.

But you have developed a talent for knowing what will function. And you know from experience that this guy is normally pretty good. In fact, he has been involved with some of your studio's most successful productions.

After setting up a time to meet, the agent sends you a synopsis of the film along with extracts from the script. He's acting on behalf of his client, a writer, and wants to sell you the rights to make a film.

After sitting through the presentation you get down to business. Yes, you are interested. You think you might be on to a winner. However, it's a tough market that's already crowded with similar projects.

The agent, who is also well experienced in these types of negotiations, starts to play his game. 'Look, if you are not interested, that's fine,' he says. 'Just let me know, I 'm meeting with two other studios this week.'

You're of two minds - you could call his bluff and let him go. However, your mind challenges you to pursue the chance which may turn out to be a great opportunity. So what do you do?

During your negotiations, the agent lays down his terms. He wants $100,000 outright for the script. With that amount comes lifetime rights to make the film. You may even sell it on if you decide not to make it yourself.

However, you do not want to pay this much money upfront. There are plenty of other scripts around that you could probably pick up for a better price.

But there's something about the film that resonates. And, you don't wish to run the risk of a competitor getting their hands on it. What if it becomes a massive hit?

So you make a counter offer.

You tell the agent that you'll give him $10,000 right away. For that money, you want exclusive rights to the film for a period of up to one year. If it doesn't go into production during this period, you agree to give up all rights at the end of the time. And, of course, they get to keep the $10,000.

However, if you do make the film during this period, you agree to pay $100,000 once it officially goes into production. Eager to make a deal, the agent agrees to these terms.

What have you done?

As the head of the movie studio, you have just agreed to take out an 'option' on the film. You have agreed to pay $10,000 for the rights to make a movie, within an agreed time frame (one year) for a set price of $100,000.

It's important to comprehend exactly what you've just paid for. It's the 'right' to make the movie. It doesn't mean you 'have' to make the movie. And you don't 'own' the movie either - not unless you pay the agent $100,000 before the option expires.

Compare this with the agent's obligations. By taking the $10,000, he has given up his rights to the movie for twelve months. Meaning that if someone else approaches him in the meantime and offers him $200,000 for example, he can't go and sell it to them instead.

Although you (as the option buyer) and the agent (as the seller) are both parties to the same transaction, you can see that your rights and obligations are very different.

And so it is with share options.

The buyer has 'rights', whilst the seller (also known as the option 'writer') has 'obligations'. The option writer must deliver the underlying commodity, be it a film script, a tonne of wheat, or an ounce of gold, if and when the buyer exercises their rights. This can happen any time up until the option expires.

Why does the option writer take on this obligation? The answer is simple - they are doing it to receive a fee. Or in option jargon, to receive the 'premium'. Once any option expires, it is worthless. Meaning that the option writer gets to bank this premium.

To receive this premium, the option writer must fulfil their obligations until either of two things happen. One, the option lapses, which occurs at the expiry date. Or two, it's exercised by the option buyer.

What are the parts that make up an option?

You can see from the movie script example that there are certain parts that combine to make up an option. These components include:

Asset - the asset over which the option is being written. In this case it's a movie script, but it could be practically anything.

Options aren't a new concept, they've been used extensively throughout history.

Fixed price - the amount that the buyer agrees to pay to the seller for the underlying asset, if and when they exercise their option. For the movie script, the agreed (or exercise) price is $100,000.

For a share option, you'll also see this called the 'strike' price.

Expiration date - which sets the deadline for the option to be exercised, otherwise it will expire worthless. In the movie example, it's one year from when they enter the option agreement.

The premium - the amount the two parties agree that the buyer pays to the seller for the option. In the above example, it's $10,000.

These are the basic parts on which both the buyer and seller must agree in any option contract. They must be clear and specific. This way both the seller and buyer understand exactly what their role is in any option contract. That is, what their specific rights (the buyer) and obligations (the seller) are while the exercise price, expiry date and the premium seem straight forward enough, the 'asset' is the one part that needs the most clarity. It needs to be clear exactly what is going to change hands if the buyer exercises their option.

Creating option contracts with clear and consistent features makes for a transparent and readily tradable market. This increases the liquidity as both buyers and sellers become confident in how the option market works.

Likewise with the ASX, share options are made up of clear and consistent parts. For example, each option contract is typically 100 shares. And each option is for a specific share, whether it be ANZ, BHP or Woodside Petroleum.

The ASX also sets a series of expiry dates for each of these share options. It is usually done in March, June, September and December. Although some, like Telstra and the bank shares have many more expiry dates than this.

Each of these expiry dates typically repeat year after year, building confidence in the consistency of the market.

There exists two different types of options, a call option and a put option.

More descriptions will be provided later in the book. For an overview, a call option provides the buyer with the capacity to purchase the underlying asset for a specific price prior to expiry. With the put option, the buyer the right to trade the underlying asset for a specific price prior to expiry.

In the example with the movie script, you as the head of the movie studio are buying a 'call' option on the movie. That is, you're buying the right to take ownership of the movie script if you choose, within the agreed time frame, for a set price.

While you are the 'call' option buyer, the agent is the seller (or writer) of the 'call' option. You are both parties to the same transaction.

Option buyers and sellers have the same rights and obligations for both call and put options. The buyer gains rights when they purchase an option. The seller takes on obligations for which they receive a fee, the premium.

The only difference is that with a call option, the buyer has the right to buy something. Whereas, with a put option, they have the right to sell something.

The Concepts Behind Options

A. Options are Derivatives

Financial instruments are a varied lot and are changing and growing all the time, sometimes rapidly. Everyone has heard about derivatives. Derivatives are simply financial instruments whose value depends on the value of some other instrument. The financial instruments commonly referred to are things like stocks, municipal bonds, notes, commercial bonds, ETF's, index funds, and so many more. Options are just another financial instrument, but they are a form of a derivative. That is, the value of the option depends on the value of the underlying financial instrument.

An option is a choice because you have the option to act on the contract or not, depending on your decisions and the market conditions. Normally, we would act on an option if the decision is in our favor and not if it is to our disadvantage. That is a strong argument for dealing in options. However, in most cases, you are not required to act on the contract, an action called execution of the option. You don't have to if you don't want to. On the other hand, if you buy an option to buy at the contract terms, the seller of that contract is required to sell under those terms. That part of options is a one-way street. Historically, only 10% of options are exercised, that is acted upon, 60% are traded before expiration and the remaining 30% expire worthless.

B. Trading in Options Has Both Risks and Rewards

Trading in options is not without risk, especially for new traders. It is remarkably easy to lose money trading in options. All it takes is a few bad decisions, which are frequently based on lack of understanding on the part of the investor or by not paying attention. We strongly recommend trading only with risk capital. That is, money you can afford to lose if things go bad. Don't trade in options with the rent money or the money set aside for the kid's college education.

This book is designed to help you avoid those mistakes by providing an introductory understanding. Can you trade in options without reading or studying the subject? Of course, but no one can speak a new language without first studying it. Same thing with options trading. This book will get you started by pointing out the fundamentals, but you, the investor, must continue to study and learn, hopefully before you start trading options. Importantly, some of the resources listed in Chapter 7 offer virtual trading platforms, in which you can trade with virtual money, not your own. This is free training and allows you to learn without losing real money. Besides, it is fun.

C. Pick Your Own Trading Strategy

Your trading strategy can be speculative, income, or conservative. A speculative strategy is based on predicting the timing and amount of any movement in the price of the stock. A conservative strategy involves trading in a manner that protects against large losses for equities the investor owns. An income strategy is one under which you generate regular income above that from normal stock gains or dividends. We will cover these in due course.

Usually, options are based on common stocks. We will follow that custom, but options are available for many different instruments like ETF's and Stock Indices. It's just easier to understand with stocks.

D. Option Trading Uses its Own Vocabulary

When you understand a few basic concepts and some vocabulary, you will see that it is not all that complicated. However, you have to study not only the market, but the ins and outs of options trading, too. Now, some of the vocabulary may seem arcane, but it is the "lingo" of Wall Street and is used by all traders and brokers everywhere. You will need to understand this vocabulary to understand the business of options trading.

E. Decide to Pay Attention

Remember, if you choose to trade in options, you have new opportunities but also new responsibilities. If you are holding options on a stock or other instrument, you must keep a close eye on it. There is nothing automatic about options. If you hold an option and it suddenly becomes very valuable, it is up to you to act on it. It will not act on its own, in fact, it may expire and you will lose the premium cost and any value of the option. Under some circumstances, you may be assigned, which means you are required to act on the option. Apart from assignments, nobody is going to call you and ask you what you want to do. You have to follow it closely, but that is interesting and sometimes, exciting.

We assume in this book that you are already familiar with trading in the stock market but somewhat new to trading in options. We can't teach you all the fundamentals of stock market trading and options trading in one book, but we can give you a peek at trading in options. We do, however, offer some information about the stock market in the context of trading in options.

Chapter 2: Basics of stock market

Let's learn how to select the correct stock options for options trading.

Step 1: Decide on the outlook of the underlying stock.

There is no magic formula in options trading where you can simply trade and profit without concern for the trend of the underlying instrument. The first step to choosing the correct option to trade comes from what you expect the underlying stock to do in the first place. There are generally only three outlooks in stock trading; bullish, bearish or neutral. However, in order to optimize profits in options trading, there can be as many as six different outlooks; sustained bullish, neutral, moderately bullish, volatile, sustained bearish and moderately bearish. You need to decide on which of these six outlooks most closely conform to your expectation on the underlying stock as each of these outlooks require a different options strategy to best optimize its profit potential.

Step 2: Decide on the time frame of that outlook.

Now that you have decided on what the underlying stock is going to do, the next question to answer is WHEN you think the underlying stock going to fulfill its expected outlook. This answers the question of which expiration month to trade your options on. One of the first things that baffle new options traders is the number of expiration months available for each stock. Options are derivative instruments that expire once its lifespan is up. It isn't like stocks which can last as long as the company remains in existence. This makes choosing the correct expiration month so important. Options become more and more expensive and less and less sensitive to movements in the underlying stock with longer expiration. This is why trading options isn't as easy as simply trading options with the longest possible expiration. If you trade options with unnecessarily long expiration, you are paying more for nothing and lowering your return on investment. Conversely, if you trade options with too short expiration, you can end up with a worthless expired position even before the underlying stock has time to move according to your prediction. As such, the more accurately you can predict when the underlying stock is going to behave the way it is expected to, the better you can optimize return on investment in options trading. There are situations such as earnings releases or some major announcements where the exact timing of the outlook can be determined. Other than such objective events, predicting when a stock is going to hit a certain price or remain within a price range requires extremely strong technical analysis skill and experience.

Step 3: Decide on the magnitude of that outlook.

The magnitude of an outlook refers to how strongly you expect the underlying stock to move in the expected direction. In the case of an expected neutral trend, magnitude refers to the expected length of that neutral trend as well as how much volatility is expected within that neutral trend. This is also why in options trading, bullish and bearish trends are classified as either sustained or moderate. Knowing the magnitude of the outlook allows you to decide on the moneyness of the option that you should trade. Moneyness refers to how much in the money or out of the money an option is. The more an option is 'in the money', the more expensive it is and the lower the leverage but the better it is at capturing profits on small price movements of the underlying stock. The more out of the money an option is, the cheaper it is, the higher the leverage and the less sensitive it is to price movements on the underlying stock, making them better for use when the expected magnitude of price movement is big.

Step 4: Decide on the optimal options strategy for your account level.

Now that you have an idea what the underlying stock might do, when it is going to do it and how powerful the movement might be, this is when you should decide on the optimal options strategy to profit from that move. The optimal options strategy could be as simple as buying a call option or put option or as complex as a Double Butterfly Spread. Your choice of options strategy would also be limited by your account trading level which defines the range of options strategy that you are allowed to perform. This options account trading level is determined by your broker on an individual basis depending on your fund size and your trading experience.

Step 5: Decide on the exact option to trade taking all of the above into consideration.

Having taken all of the above factors into consideration, you would then be able to decide on the exact correct option to trade. Here's an example of how it works:

Assuming it is currently January and the price of a stock is $50. Assuming you think the price of that stock is going to move upwards but only moderately up to $55 by next month. You decided that this is a moderately bullish outlook which can be better optimized using a Bull Call Spread, writing out of the money call options on the expected price ceiling on at the money call options, rather than just buying in the money call options and your account trading level allows you to execute such debit spreads. Taking all of these factors into consideration, you decided to execute a 50/55 bull call spread on that stock's March expiration options, giving a little bit more time for the stock to move to that expected price.

Chapter 3: Technical and fundamental analysis

Forex trading is not as complex as you think it is. In fact, it is quite easy if you know what to do.

Technical analysis

The technical analysis of forex deals with indulging in some heavy-duty mathematics and statistics. It is comparable to the approach that is taken towards calculating the technical analysis related to the stock market. There are a few complex equations that you should calculate, and they are discussed as under.

Moving averages

This is using the power of the trend to assess the direction of the market. As you know, it is extremely important for you to be able to predict how the value of the currency will move next. For this, it is best to go through the different trends that the value of the currency has been following in the recent past. The basic idea is to trace the trend that the price has been following. How is it moving ahead, where does the price reversal point lie, at what point is it most profitable to sell the currency, etc.?

You have to take a series of price points, add them all together and then divide them by the total number of price points. This is a very basic method yet quite effective. The next type is the weighted moving average method. In this method, you assign the rates numbers based on the time when they were calculated. The oldest one receives 1 and so on. The third method is the exponential moving average method and involves extreme mathematical calculations, which goes beyond the scope of this book.

Forex hedging against inflation

It is obvious that every investor will worry about the inflation at some point in time or the other. For this, the trader can indulge in hedging. Hedging refers to protecting the investment from potential future losses. The trader will buy an asset that is priced much higher. That way, even if the value of the currency decreases then the trader can safeguard the investment. Forex is often compared with gold investments as the two provide similar protection against inflation.

Bollinger bands

Bollinger bands are the next technical analysis that you must run your currency pair through. This type was developed by John Bollinger. It involves understanding the real-time volatility that a pair of currencies will go through. Just like the moving averages, here too, there are certain situations where you have to employ this technique to arrive at the appropriate results. For example, you have to use at the standard deviations as a tool to measure the pattern of fluctuations in the currency pair. Similarly, you have to use other statistical tools and use it in relation to the Bollinger bands to arrive at a particular trend.

Relative strength index

The relative strength index is a great statistical tool that you can use to check whether a currency is valued at the right price or over or under valued. It is important for you to check this, as you need to buy a currency that is valued at the right price. Once you apply this technique on the trend of the currency, you will find a number. If the number is 30 or under then the currency is oversold, and if it is 70 or higher then it means that it is overbought. Both of these can be a bad thing for any currency. So you have to steer clear off of them and look for pairs that lie in between. The calculation of RSI is generally seen as a tedious task. But the good news is that there are many software available that will easily and quickly calculate the amount for you without having to put in too much effort towards.

Fibonacci retracements

If you are aware of the Fibonacci number sequence, then you will find this technique easy to adopt. It makes use of the Fibonacci number sequence to find the trend that the currency will follow. It is a predictive approach and is meant to help to understand whether or not the currency pairs will prove to be a lucrative investment.

These form the different technical analysis that you can perform to understand the trend of the currencies.

Stochastic oscillator

The stochastic oscillator is a system that you can use to look at the difference in prices of currency and use a scale to measure it. This too requires you to conduct an in-depth statistical calculation which you can easily do using a simple software. The software will give you a quick result, and you won't have to do all the calculations.

Sentimental analysis

Sentimental analysis refers to understanding the sentiment of the investors in the market. You have to analyze their mood and see what they are thinking about a certain currency. Whether they are interested in buying it or they wish to steer clear of it. You have to understand the course that they will take in order to make your own decision. In general, you have to follow the crowd if you wish to make a safe investment. But if you want to do something different then you should move against the crowd.

Fundamental analysis

Now those of you that are stock market experts will be aware of the fundamental and technical analysis that is conducted on stocks. It involves looking at the company's background, calculating the P/E ratio, calculating the return on investment ratio, etc. All of these are calculated to check whether a particular stock is undervalued and to quickly invest in it.

But this system only works in the stock market and not the forex market. The fundamental analysis that is conducted in the forex market is much different.

Although they are both known as fundamental analysis, they take into consideration different factors.

In the forex market, the fundamental analysis refers to studying the economic conditions that prevail in the individual countries in order to understand their impact on currency fluctuations. Let us look at some of the factors that you have to understand in detail if you wish to conduct this type of analysis on the currencies.

Employment

The employment scenario of a country determines the value of the local currency. As you know, if a person is employed then he or she will have the power to buy more. This will impact the value of the currency. It ends up affecting inflation, and this will cause the value of the currency to rise. For this, you have to look at the number of employed and number of unemployed people. If the employed is more than the unemployed, then the prices will be stable. But if there is a wave of layoffs then the value of the currency will be affected.

Weather conditions

Sometimes, extreme weather conditions or natural calamities also have an impact on the rate of the currency. You have to watch the news to know about these and see if they really are impacting the value of the country's currency.

These form the different things that you should look into to see if the value of a particular country's currency would rise or fall.

GDP

GDP refers to the gross domestic product. Gross domestic product refers to how much the nation is earning collectively. This includes per capita income and also the consumer price index. You have to study these two factors of a company if you wish to understand how much they are earning and how it will affect the value of the currency. Some countries think of it as a good thing for the GDP to rise, as it will indicate the economic stability that prevails in the country. However, if the GDP rises then it also means that the value of the goods in the country is rising which makes it a bad thing for the economy of the country.

Interest rates

The very first factor that influences the currency rates is the interest rates. The interest rates that prevail in a particular country are always controlled by the country's central bank. The interest rates control the currency values to a very large extent. In fact, it has been observed that mere rumors of changes in the interest rates have generated a lot of movement in the forex markets. The two are that closely knit and go hand in hand. So, in order to know whether or not the rates will be affected by the economic makeup of a country, you have to keep an eye on the interest rates.

Prices of commodities

The prices of commodities will have a direct bearing on the country's currency value. You have to look at the prices that basic goods are sold at. They will help you determine whether or not the value of the currency will remain stable or fluctuate. You have to read the news regularly and see if there is any movement in the prices of these commodities. If so, is there news of it affecting the economic situation in the country? These are the questions that will have to be asked and answered to arrive at the answer.

Chapter 4: Trading Strategies for different asset classes

Why Do You Need a Plan?

An important part of any new venture that you want to start is to have a detailed plan for the task at hand. Why would trading be any different from any other venture in your life? A trading strategy must state what you want to accomplish and the reason for doing so. A strategic plan will be a review of your abilities, skills, the resources at your disposal, and your expectations. The strategy will serve as a compass that will help you in coming up with a trading plan that will be profitable.

A trading strategy will help you in defining the "what" and the "why" that has gotten you into trading in the first place. It will help you in outlining the steps that you need to take while evaluating, executing, and managing your investments. You will need to think about a few things before you can develop your strategy for trading. Do you have an existing strategy? Do you know the reason why you want to trade? What is success, according to you, and how do you plan on achieving your goals? With the help of a strategic plan, you will be able to achieve them.

However, having a trading strategy doesn't guarantee success. You will need to be able to develop one that will help you in understanding your motivations and goals and then implement it if you want to make it big in investing. So how do you create a trading strategy, and how does this help in binary options trading? In this chapter, you will learn about the importance of a trading strategy and the method of developing your trading strategy.

There is a difference in being proactive and reactive. With a strategic plan for investing, you can make sure that you are proactive instead of reactive. You can make your future happen instead of just waiting for it to happen. You no longer have to be a victim of circumstances. It isn't possible to foresee all the changes that the market might undergo; however, you don't have to worry about being caught off-guard if you have a plan in place. You can prepare for contingencies and minimize the damage that you might suffer. If you have a strategic plan, then you will know the manner in which you are supposed to react in case things don't turn out the way they were supposed to. You will have a sense of direction.

How do you differentiate between a good and a great idea? Without a clear idea of what you want to achieve and the reason for which you are doing it, everything will certainly seem like a good idea. What are you supposed to invest in and how much must your investment be? Having some clarity about what you want to do and how to do it will help you in making better use of your resources, especially the most important resources at your disposal—your time, effort, and money. You will be able to make an informed decision instead of an impulsive one. Impulsive decisions might not always pay you well. Having a trading strategy will help minimize risk. It is impossible to avoid risk altogether, but you can certainly reduce your exposure to risk by planning. It will also help in increasing your profitability.

The one thing that you need to keep in mind while planning is to understand that patience is a key virtue. Your investments might not give you overnight profits, so be patient. Your efforts will certainly pay off, if not immediately, eventually.

Before you can get started with developing a plan for investing, you will need to consider a few things.

What do you want to accomplish? Do you want to start investing to get better control of your finances? Do you want to be able to generate a supplementary income? Do you want to create a fund for a rainy day or your retirement? Defining what you want to accomplish will influence your investing decisions. Once you have figured out what the motivational factor is, the next step will be to decide your level of risk tolerance. Do you like taking risks or are you averse to them? Will your orientation towards risk dictate your investing decisions? How will assuming more risk affect other aspects of your life? Once you have figured both of these things out, the next step is to identify the challenges that stand in your way. Most often than not, one of the major challenges that you might encounter will be a time crunch. There can be other challenges like lack of resources or knowledge.

Three Types of Strategies

You can make decisions based on your gut instinct, and you don't need a trading strategy; however, if you want to be a successful trader, then this sort of approach will not be helpful. It might have the opposite effect. If you want to be a successful and profitable trader, then you need a binary options trading strategy. There are three different types of strategies that every trader needs, and they are as follows.

Trading Strategies

There are two primary reasons why you must follow a trading strategy. A trading strategy helps eliminate the likelihood of making emotional or irrational decisions while trading. Instead, it allows you to work with preset parameters that are based on rationality and applicability. The second reason is that a trading strategy helps you to benefit from repetition. Without a trading strategy, it will be difficult to determine what worked and why. Even if you can determine these answers, it will be impossible to repeat the same. A trading strategy helps to ensure that your trades are always based on logical and practical thinking while ensuring that you keep track of the pattern that you can repeat, analyze, or adjust later.

For instance, you can analyze a specific strategy after conducting a certain number of trades or after the expiry of a set time frame. Is the strategy profitable? Are you able to earn decent profits? Maybe the strategy is helping you earn money, but it isn't as much as you hoped for. In such a situation, you can either decide to test whether the strategy's profitability will increase in the long run, or you might want to make certain changes to the strategy to improve your earnings. This is possible only if you have a trading strategy in place.

The lack of a trading strategy will result in trading that's not only haphazard but is quite difficult to optimize as well. Without a trading strategy in place, even after a set number of trades or a time frame, you cannot gauge your performance because you have nothing to compare it to. What will you do if you lose your money? All you can do is hope that you make better decisions in the future; however, you will not have anything concrete to base any changes on. The same stands true even if you are earning money, but not as much as you hoped for. It stands true even if you make money; you have no possible way of discerning the strategy that you used to make money, and you cannot replicate it again. Every transaction will be a standalone trade, and it isn't part of your overall strategy. This is not a practical way of trading.

Let us look at a scenario where you don't have a trading plan. In this situation, you manage to make a 50 percent profit one month and then a loss of 50 percent the next. How will you know why a specific month was more successful than the other? How will you be able to determine the changes that you need to make? You will not be able to discern all this.

Money-Management Strategies

A lot of people seem to make the mistake of coming up with a trading strategy and nothing else. A trading strategy helps determine the type of asset you want to trade and your total level of risk exposure. Little or no thought is given to money management. A money-management strategy will help you optimize your balance so that you can overcome any losing streak and optimize your ability to earn.

Let us take a look at a trader who doesn't have a money-management strategy. The trader decides to invest 10 percent of his account's balance on each trade. If that trade goes bad, then he will need to make a gain of 20 percent to recover his loss and break even. If the trader loses three consecutive trades, then, to break even, the trader needs to make a profit of 30 percent. You will notice that this can creep up easily and a losing streak can empty your account within no time. In this scenario, with three unsuccessful trades, the trader loses 30 percent of the account balance. When you take into account that a lot of losing streaks last for longer than three trades, you will learn to appreciate how helpful money management is.

Without a money-management strategy, your account balance can easily be emptied, even when you have a good trading strategy in place. Losing streaks, as well as unprofitable trades, are a part of trading. So, if you have a strategy on hand, then you will be better equipped to deal with such inevitabilities. With money management, you will be able to optimize your profits, restrict your losses, and learn to recover an advantageous position after a rough patch.

Analysis and Improvement Strategies

When it comes to binary options trading strategies, there is no such thing as the perfect strategy. Markets are forever dynamic, and all successful traders need to stay on top of their game by continuously working to improve, enhance, and update their trading strategies. Even veteran traders need to analyze and improve the way they trade if they want to stay profitable. This applies to new traders as well.

An analysis and improvement strategy gives the trader a structured method of optimizing the good parts of their trading and money-management strategies. So, this strategy ensures that the previous two strategies stay effective and efficient. Since the market is dynamic and ever-changing, the strategies that you use cannot stay the same. It also helps you to adjust better to the changing market scenarios.

Without this strategy, you will merely be plodding along. If you have a great strategy in place, then you can probably make some money, but this isn't guaranteed. Even if you make money, it might not be as much as you possibly can. Why do you want to let go of the potential profits? To prevent this from happening, you need analysis and improvement strategies.

Elements of Binary Options Strategies

Three elements are common to all binary options trading strategies, and they are as follows.

Step 1 – Create signals

A signal is an indication that the price of an asset is moving in a particular direction. Of course, asset prices are constantly changing. What you need is something that predicts this movement before it happens. That makes the signal.

There are two ways to generate signals. The first is the use of news and the second is technical analysis.

It contains an analysis of the events in the news, e.g., announcing a company, announcing the industry, and publishing government inflation data.

As a result, you will find inexpensive calendars on most of the good binary options trading platforms. Knowing that a company's profit and loss account must be submitted within two days enables you to plan your analysis and trading operations in the area.

The best platforms will also show you what to expect from a news event. For example, it is useful to know that a company's earnings report should be submitted in two days, but even more useful if you know what the market expects in this report. Then you can decide on the report and try to predict the content and subsequent market movements. You can also make decisions based on expectations and market reactions after publishing.

There are positive news events in the trading approach; most importantly, it is easy to understand and analyze. This approach has disadvantages. You may consider it to be positive news event at first reading, to have a positive market reaction; however, the report may contain additional information that scares the market. For example, profits are not as high as expected. This may mean that the market moves less than expected, and in some cases, even in the wrong direction—prices fall even though the news event is considered positive.

It isn't easy to predict how long the movement will last and how far it will go. If you look back at the example of the company's income statement, this will be a positive report, so the company's stock prices are likely to rise. But how long does the situation take with price increases and when will the price reach a maximum? These questions are unknown.

Trade based on technical analysis offers an alternative. This strategy aims to predict the evolution of asset prices, regardless of what happens in the broader market.

Essentially, this process is about seeing how the price of a particular asset has moved in the past. On this basis, it is possible to determine patterns by which price movements can be predicted in the future.

It sounds difficult, but our brain is used to doing it daily; like when you meet a new person who is warm and welcoming, you will most likely predict positive things in the relationship. On the other hand, if a person is discreet or unfriendly, you can foresee difficulties in a relationship. You come to these conclusions because of your experience in meeting people and building relationships.

The technical analysis does something similar. It looks at the current state of assets and decides, by experience, whether the price remains largely unchanged or is growing or falling.

Understanding technical terms and concepts can be a bit difficult. The overall concept, however, coincides with the daily task of predicting future results based on past events.

Now to the big question—should you use the message trading approach or the technical analysis approach? It depends on many factors, and the answer will be different for everyone. The best advice is to find out which one works best for you and which one makes the most profit. Of course, you cannot test strategies with your hard-earned money.

The last point to consider when looking at signals and strategies is the short-term focus. The goal of investment strategies is to predict the price evolution of an asset over a long period, such as over 10 years. This type of information is not used when trading binary options. Instead, you need to know if the price will move in the next few minutes, the next hour, or the next day. The price forecast after 10 years is not relevant.

For this, you need short-term signals and short-term strategies.

Step 2 – How much should you trade?

Essentially, this is a money-management strategy. They vary in complexity and success, starting with the strategy of making the same amount for each transaction. Martingale strategy and percentage strategy are two other strategies. For long-term success, the last option is the best.

Investing the same amount of money in each transaction is synonymous with no strategy. This is the riskiest strategy as it does not take into account either the overall profitability or the amount of money you have in your account. Both are important factors that, if ignored, can quickly exhaust the balance.

Let's look at two more general strategies, starting with Martingale's capital management strategy.

The main concept of the Martingale strategy is to recover losses as quickly as possible. This means that, after a lost trade, large amounts of money must be invested in transactions. For example, you may have a fixed value of the money you trade, which you double when you make a loss. If this deal wins, you will return to winning and not near the breakeven.

Problems with this strategy arise when you have multiple losing trades in a row. Any loss-making transaction in the Martingale strategy implies an increase in investment in the next transaction. That adds up quickly. For example, imagine you have a loss of 10 deals. That's a lot, but it's not an unrealistic or unreasonable situation. If you lose 10 trades, your 11th trade must be 1024 times your original trade to stay in the Martingale system. There are not many budgets that can withstand such an increase, even if the cost of the original transaction was low.

The question is how accurate your predictions are and whether you can prevent or minimize the number of lost trades. It's always important to know that trading binary options is not a reliable thing.

The percentage system is less risky and is therefore preferred by most traders, especially those unfamiliar with binary options trading. The concept is pretty simple— the amount invested in the transaction depends on the balance of your account. If you lose the transaction, your account balance will decrease, reducing the amount invested in the next transaction. On the other hand, if you win a trade, the amount of money that will be invested in the next trade increases because your balance has increased.

This strategy helps to keep your balance unchanged so that you can make a steady profit over time.

Then the question arises as to what percentage of your credit you want to invest. As a guide, a trader who feels a risk may choose a figure of about five percent, while a trader who likes no risk chooses a value of about two percent.

For example, suppose you invest five percent of your account balance. With a $500 balance, your transactions would be $25. If your account balance drops to $300, your transactions will also decrease— each investment will cost you $15. In contrast, if your balance increases to $800, each of your transactions will be $40.

This is a strategy that only lets you invest the amount you can afford. This is a strategy to increase your profits and protect your balance even in difficult times or during a losing streak.

Step 3 – Improve your strategy

You can do this by analyzing your results using a diary. This is a simple but very effective concept.

This includes keeping a journal in which you record every transaction you have made. Then you can search for patterns and trends to see what works and what does not.

This is especially effective if you are new and still trying to develop a profitable strategy. The general approach in this scenario is to place trades with technical analysis signals and message-event signals. A diary helps you to split these offers so that you can judge which ones were better. For example, you may find that you are gaining twice the value of transactions that you receive as a result of the technical analysis. From experience, however, you know that you spend more time with the signals of messages than with the technical analysis. The information in your journal indicates that you should consider changing the approach.

Everything depends on which deals work and which do not. The only way to do that is to keep records, so the trading diary is a very effective tool.

In a trading diary, you can also focus on details to optimize your overall trading strategy. In the end, you reach the point where you want to increase your profitability by one or two percentage points. It is simply impossible to act sustainably if you do not keep good records. On the other hand, successful completion of this task can lead to additional profits of hundreds or even thousands of dollars.

Remember to use your trade journal to check all parts of your trading approach, not just your trading strategy. This includes how to manage money and how to determine the value of each transaction. This includes finding the best benefits for your purchase and style.

Then you can go into detail. For example, you can see the best days of the week or the best times of the day. This information may help you to customize your approach. You can also see which brokers work best for you and more.

A trade diary will tell you a lot of things. Working with too many people at the same time can be a problem. When you do this, you do not know which changes beneficial and which ones will be will not. The easiest way to fix this is to focus on individual changes, analyze their effects, and then proceed. Again, your trade diary is critical to this process.

If you do not keep a trade journal, start as soon as possible. It becomes an indispensable tool.

Strategies

When trading binary options, there are various assets to choose from. The oldest and most effective approach to minimizing risk, however, is to focus on a single asset. Trade the assets you know best, such as Euro-dollar rates. Consistent trading helps you get used to it, and forecasting of the value direction becomes easier. Below are two types of strategies that can be of great value when trading binary options.

Trend strategy

When a flat trend line is predicted, the price of the assets will rise, it is then recommended to use the option without touch.

If the trend line indicates that the asset is growing, select CALL.

If the trend line indicates a decrease in the investment price, select PUT.

Pinocchio Strategy

This strategy is used when it is expected that the price of an asset will rise sharply or go in the opposite direction. If a value is expected to increase, select CALL, and if it is expected to drop, select PUT. This is best done on a broker's free demo account.

Straddle Strategy

Apply this strategy when the market is volatile or right before the release of important news on specific stocks or when analysts' forecasts are afloat. This is a highly valued strategy used in the global trading community. This strategy is best known to allow the trader to avoid selecting the options CALL and PUT, instead placing both on the selected asset.

The general idea is to use PUT when the value of an asset increases, but there are signs or assumptions that this value will soon fall. Once a deviation occurs, place the CALL option on it and expect it to return to normal soon. This can also be done in the opposite direction by providing CALL with CALL at a low price and with the increasing value of the PUT assets. This significantly increases the chances of success in at least one of the trading options and leads to a result "in money." A straddle strategy is highly valued by traders as the market grows and falls or when a particular asset has a volatile value.

Risk-reduction strategy

This is truly one of the most respected strategies by experienced binary options traders around the world. The goal is to reduce the risk factor of trading and increase the chances of a successful outcome, which leads to a positive increase in profits. This strategy is implemented by placing the CALL and PUT options concurrently on a separate basis. This is especially useful when trading assets with fluctuating values. Of course, binary options can have two possible outcomes. Trading two opposing forecasts simultaneously for a single asset ensures that at least one of them achieves a positive outcome.

Hedging strategy

This strategy is commonly referred to as "pairing" and is mostly used in conjunction with binary options companies, investors, and traditional exchanges to protect and minimize the risks involved. This strategy is implemented by placing the call and the put simultaneously in the same asset. This ensures that, regardless of the direction of the value of the asset, the transaction results in a successful outcome. This gives the investor a profit in the result "in money."

Basic analysis

This strategy is used primarily in stock trading and, above all, by traders to better understand the asset they choose. This increases their accuracy chances in predicting future price changes. This approach involves a thorough review of all of the company's financials. This information should include income reports, financial statements and market shares

This assessment helps the trader understand the past activity of the asset and its response to specific financial fluctuations in a better manner. It helps them make strong predictions in future trading strategies under known circumstances. Note that with a good binary trading robot, you can completely skip these steps.

Failing to plan means that you are planning to fail, and there before starting off a binary options trader, you must devise a trading strategy. Use the list of elements given in this chapter will help you come up with a trading strategy that'll improve your chances of succeeding as a trader.

Chapter 5: Starting Forex Trading

Before you can start doing forex trading, you must understand what it is. Stock trading lets one select the number of stocks they want to buy or sell, but forex trading is different because you trade with currency. It is difficult to decide to sell 7000 Euros. The bottom line is one lot that represents 100,000 units of base currency. As such, you can choose how much base currency you want to invest. There is no need to have too much money in your account because you can use leverage.

Why many people lose money in Forex?

Let's find out a few reasons why many people lose money in Forex. First, they don't know how to use leverage. Leverage is an excellent technique, but at the same time, dangerous when you trade on Forex.

One reason why leverage is compelling is that, with just a few bucks, you can open trading positions worth $100,000 of dollars. If you are right in your trade, then you'll make a big profit. Conversely, if you are wrong, you might lose all your money.

For that reason, traders are advised to start small. You can start with micro lots or nano lots. The same way, it is risky to invest in the stock market with real money worth; the same applies to Forex trading.

Start small

You can't get rich fast by just trading in micro lots, but it will protect your trading positions because you have the opportunity to learn from live trading. Some of the reasons why most traders lose all their money in Forex are because:

- They start with a small trading capital and expect to make thousands of dollars in a short period.

- They open huge trading positions, but they don't understand leverage.

When you want to trade small, you must first check whether a broker offers trade sizes as small as nano lots or micro lots.

Steps to start forex trading

Now you know what pips, lots, and leverage are; you have a basic understanding of forex trading. What next then?

Step 1: Choose a Forex Broker

The first step in trading forex is to select your forex broker. Nowadays, there are many forex brokers, and this can be difficult to pick the best one. Don't forget that many brokers provide a demo account for one to test their trading platform.

When it comes to choosing a broker, the first thing you should do is to research with the aim to find out whether a broker has a good reputation and whether they can fulfill your needs. Since many brokers offer a demo account to test their services, one is advised to test out as many platforms as you can before you choose on a broker. Below are some tips to help you pick a good Forex broker.

1. Regulatory compliance

Regulatory compliance is the first thing to consider. You must be a National Futures Association (NFA) member to be considered as a trusted forex broker in the United States.. Instead, a broker that belongs to the National Futures Association as declared in the CFTC regulations will display its NFA member number on the website. Since forex trading involves money, and there is a risk of fraud, traders are advised to open accounts with brokers that have a full regulation.

2. Account details

Each forex broker will offer an account that comes with:

- Spreads and Commission. Commission and spreads are where a broker can make money. If a commission is used by a broker, they may choose to charge a specific amount of the spread. Many brokers like to advertise that they charge no commission, but they offer money with wider spreads. When the spread is vast, it becomes more difficult for a trader to make a profit. Major trading currency pairs such as EUR/USD have a stronger spread than other minor traded currency pairs.

- Initial deposits and withdrawals. Every Forex broker has a customized policy to guide on funding and account withdrawal. Account holders are allowed by a broker to receive funds online via Paypal or credit card. The broker can then charge a specific fee for each service.

3. The type of currency pairs offered

While there is a good currency deal in forex trading, only a few deals have the most attention. Apart from the major currency pairs, a broker can have other forex pairs. All in all, brokers provide you with currency pairs that you can use to trade.

4. Customer Service

You know that Forex trading is a 24-hour activity. For that reason, best forex brokers should have their customer support team available for 24-hours. Additionally, it should be easy for traders to speak with a live customer support staff. Traders should not hang on a phone call for a long time or speak with an auto attendant. When looking for a reliable broker, you can try to call the customer service to find out how quick they are in answering a call. If they pick your call without having to wait for a long time, it shows that they are reliable. You should also find out how experienced the customer support staff is in answering questions to do with leverage, spread, and regulations. Find out the length of period they have been in the forex market.

5. Trading Platform

An investor's portal in the market can be compared to a trading platform. That is why traders should verify that the software and platform are easy to use. The platform should have all the technical tools that traders require to use to control their trade positions. Also, it should be easy for traders to enter and exit trades. An excellent trading platform has "buy" and "sell" buttons. Others have a "panic" button that turns off open trading positions. A poor trading interface may make a trader to make mistakes such as closing a trade position instead of opening.

Other factors include trading alerts, customization options, automated trading options, and the type of order entry.

The Bottom Line

If you have a trusted broker, you'll devote more attention and time to building your forex strategy. Doing a little research before picking a broker increases the odds of success of an investor in the competitive forex market.

Step 2: Install Trading Software

Once you pick your broker, the next thing is to install trading software. Trading software allows investors to make stock decisions regarding fundamental analysis and technical analysis. Stock market trading software is used by traders to select shares.

Features of a Trading Software

1. Trading software should be flexible and allow traders to personalize many different items on their charts like comparisons, indicators, and many more. The most important thing is to save all your customizations. This is something that websites don't support, and you have to edit your indicators any time you look at a different stock.

2. Trading software should allow you to enter your formula for choosing stocks. In other words, you can filter out your stock based on your set criteria.

3. Software should make it easy for you to switch between stocks. If you use a website that offers similar services, it will take more time to scan ten different stocks.

The main benefit of using trading software is that it saves much time. Time is critical because if you have another job, you will only set aside a few hours each day to trade and earn extra income on the stock market.

Types of Trading Software

Some of the most common features include:

- Placing trades

- Programmatic Trading

- Fundamental analysis

- Paper trading

- Technical analysis

Before you make any decisions on trading software, traders and investors should carefully analyze the features they need. Active traders who depend on automated trading systems may select different trading software than an investor who is looking for the ability to place trades. Additionally, these software applications may contain different fee structures, performance features, and other factors that affect profitability. It is crucial for traders to consider all these factors before they make any decision to help them optimize their profits.

Finding your Forex Account

Once you have registered a forex account, the next thing is to deposit funds. That should be easy. Start with a minimum of $100 but note that brokers have their minimum amount.

Test the Platform using a Demo Account

Before you make any decision to open a real account, it's essential to test a platform on a demo account. A demo account has virtual currency for you to test different strategies. Try it out to experience how placing stop loss works. Don't switch to a real account and start to test everything for the first time.

Making a profit in Forex is not easy, and that is why you should take time to practice a lot on a demo account. Don't be in a rush. Take time to master a few trading skills and how you can trade smart.

That said, what is the best way of trading? Should one use simulators or paper trading?

Well, paper trading is a great way to trade with virtual money. A few years before the release of simulators, you had to use a piece of paper to analyze your trades. Once you felt confident, then you can switch on a real account. During this period, it was expensive to open and close a trade. Paper trading was the best option because traders could learn how to trade without using real money.

Over time, trading simulators became the new version of paper trading. Although you could still use a pencil and paper to trade, using simulators was far easier.

Advantages of Forex Demo Trading

There are a few advantages when you decide to trade on a forex demo account before switching to actual trading. The main advantages include:

- You don't risk your real cash. Losses and gains are virtual. Thus, you can't lose your trading capital.

- You get a chance to test a trading system and trading strategies.

Disadvantages of Demo Trading

- You don't get a chance to react if you were trading on real cash.

- You open trades that you can't do so when using real cash to trade.

So is demo trading the best way to use to learn to trade?

Of course, the answer is yes. If you are not confident enough to trade on real cash or you doubt a particular trading strategy, then demo trading is the best to use to clear those doubts.

Trading on a demo account is better especially when you are about to start to trade on real cash. The currency market has leverage. When using leverage, you can open different trading position. If you like, you can open a trading position that is as big as 10 lots or the least position of 1 lot. Positions smaller than 1 are micro lots. If you find it strange, then you should test it on a demo account. The most important thing to remember is that leverage can make you lose all your money in the account in just a few minutes of opening trade. For that reason, you should know how to control the size of your trade position and understand how it works. Depending on the way you use leverage, you can either make a huge profit or terrible losses.

Demo trading is not at all a wrong thing, but in the long-term is not the best method to use to learn to trade. You must use a real account with small cash.

Trading and Psychology

After you have traded on a demo account and then you switch to actual trading, the first thing that you will realize is the difference between demo trading and real money trading. First, you will want to be careful so that you don't lose your money. You will not jump quickly into opening trades with leverage position as you did in the demo account. You'll discover that before you start any trading position, you will give it a second thought.

Besides that, when you are making a profit, you will not want to close the trade because you think the profit may increase. These are just a few of the emotions that you will experience with real money trading. With time, you start to understand that most losses in forex are because traders don't have a trading plan. Many traders allow emotions to control them in making decisions.

You will have a big problem to control your emotions. However, as a trader, you must be aware of your feelings and not give it a chance to control your trading decisions. That is why you are advised to create a trading plan on paper. The plan should have many things that will help you become a better trader.

Learning to Trade on Forex

So far, you know the basics of forex trading. However, how can one learn how to trade well in the forex market? Luckily, there are a few tips to help you become a better forex trader.

Look for a Mentor

Finding a mentor who can guide you to learn how to trade in forex and make a profit is not that easy. In fact, it is rare to find ads or information about forex mentoring. So you have the biggest task. If you have a trader that you follow, then you can decide to ask him whether they can be your mentor. Some may refuse because they don't have that time. Others may decline because they don't have the skills to mentor. Regardless of all these challenges, a mentor is the right person to help you learn how to trade in Forex. A mentor will guide you while you trade so that you don't make glaring mistakes that should affect you.

That said; look for a mentor who has gained a few skills and knowledge in the forex market. It is not the role of a mentor to teach you the basics of forex trading. Instead, a mentor should help you learn how to trade successfully.

Another thing to consider before picking a mentor is to identify your favorite trading style that you want to learn. That means if you prefer technical analysis; look for a mentor who trades using this technique. Your goal should be to learn how to trade long-term and not short-term. That is why you should not waste time looking for help from day traders, always go for long-term investors.

Learn To Trade on a Demo Account

Much has been discussed about using a demo trading account. To reinforce whatever was said before, the best way to test a new trading strategy is on a demo account. If it is your first time to forex trade, use a demo account to learn how leverage works. Find out how a spread changes for different forex pairs.

Read Trading Resources

Forex trading knowledge is crucial for one to thrive in forex trade. Reading trading books helps you develop better ideas on how to trade forex. When you learn a trading idea, you must practice it in the live market.

Watch Webinars

There are a few great free webinars. Besides this, you'll find webinars organized by certain forex brokers. A few of these webinars feature technical analysis while others are about fundamental analysis.

Enroll for a Course

The one fact about forex trading is that most traders are losing money daily. Brokers know this, and that is why some have a free trading course. Successful traders teach most of these courses. Of course, not all classes are free. There are some that you have to pay a certain fee before you get permission to access it. The choice is all yours whether you want to pay for it or not.

Follow Other Traders on Social Networks

The modern era features social networks. These are great places to chat with your fellow traders. Some of these networks feature valuable information that is good for a new trader. If you are on Twitter, look for traders using the hashtags and other keywords. In most of these social networks, you'll find traders who are ready to share out their thoughts about the current market. Sometimes, they may tweet or post interesting chart or link.

Forums

Most forums have people who talk bullshit. Well, if you like discussions, then join them. Maybe you could be lucky to find good traders who can guide you to become a better trader.

What is the bottom line?

The best lesson is that there is no single trading technique. It is your role to build your trading system. With time, you have to change the way of trading. To be successful, you must be ready to learn from other successful traders. Copy what they do. That way, there is hope for you to make it in forex trading.

Basics of Forex Trading

If you have started reading about forex trading, you most probably have heard the terms bid-ask or bid-offer. These terms are basically price quotes used for currency pairs. When trading forex, all currencies are paired with another currency, and the quotes that you will get are also double where one represents the quote for buying and another for selling. The difference between the two quotes or prices is what we refer to as the "spread." In this chapter, you will learn the basic procedures for trading in the forex market.

Forex Trading Positions

A lot of people enter forex trading in order to earn extra income and to diversify their existing investment portfolios. They are able to achieve these goals by taking positions to buy and sell varying sets of currencies. When the price of a currency increases after you have purchased it at a lesser price, you can earn your income when you "close" the position, or sell your currencies at a higher price. When you close your position, or the working order, you are technically putting up for sale the base currency that you originally bought, and you are purchasing its matching currency. This transaction involves a correlation of relative worth since the worth of one of the currencies in the pair is evaluated against the worth of the other currency. Because of this, a particular currency will only have its worth as a consequence of its correlation with another currency from another nation.

The "position" or "order" that you will open in the forex market will represent your net amount of exposure in a specific currency and in its corresponding currency pair. Your position can be described as "flat" when you basically have zero or no exposure, "long" if you are buying more currency than selling them, and "short" if you are selling more currency than buying them. When you start trading in forex, you are basically trading one currency for a different currency because you expect that the currency you bought will increase in value as compared to the value of the currency that you sold.

One of the basic forex concepts that you need to fully understand is that currencies are always traded in pairs. When you perform a trade, you are concurrently purchasing one currency which is the "base currency" (the 1st currency in the pair quote) and selling another currency which is the "quote currency" (the 2nd currency in the pair quote). You can make your profit a "realized income" by selling back the currency that you originally bought at an increased price, but you also have the option of holding your position and choosing to realize your income at a later period of time. In this case, you will have an "open position."

When you buy a specific currency pair, you are technically buying a specific amount of the base currency and selling the equivalent amount of the quote currency. This transaction is also referred to as "going long" or "longing the market." For instance, if you go long 100,000 units in the USD/EUR pair, it means that you are buying 100,000 units of the US dollar (the base currency) and selling the corresponding amount in Euro (the quote currency). If the price you were quote was 1.40 for

USD/EUR, you are basically selling 140,000 units of the Euro. When you sell the corresponding Euro amount, you are guaranteeing the purchase of the USD counterpart.

The same rule applies to the reverse position which is also referred to as "shorting the market" or "going short." When you go short on a specific base currency, you observe that the value of the base currency is declining compared to the value of the quote currency. Because of that, you will then decide to sell, for instance, the 100,000 units of US dollars that you originally bought and purchase back the 140,000 units of Euro, because you anticipate that the value of the US dollar will eventually decline and you would want to purchase it back at a lower Euro price afterwards to realize your profits.

To summarize: a position is long when you are buying a particular currency, and a position is short when you are selling that same currency. Here is another forex trading concept you need to understand: forex quotes are also usually given as pairs of bid and ask. Long forex positions (or when you are buying a currency) apply the "ask" (offer) price in the quote. For instance, if you want to purchase one standard lot of CHF/USD at a quoted rate of 1.5722 bid/1.5727 ask, it implies that you will be purchasing 100,000 units of CHF at 1.5727 US dollar. On the other hand, short forex positions (or when you are selling a currency) will apply the "bid" price in the quote. Using the same example, that means that you will be selling 100,000 units of CHF at 1.5722 US dollars.

Forex trading involves the simultaneous and symmetrical buying and selling of currency pairs. This means that you will always be long (buying) in one particular currency and short (selling) in another corresponding currency at the same time. In the above instance, if you trade your 100,000 CHF at 1.5722 US dollars, it means that you will be short (selling) in Swiss Francs (or CHF) and long (buying) in US dollars.

When you choose to keep your position open (running or active), it means that its worth will always vary depending on how the market rates fluctuate. Your position may have profits when the prices go up or losses when the prices go down, but those profits and loss will not be final or realized until you decide to close your position.

How to Trade on Margin

You can compare trading on margin by opening a loan account from a banking institution or broker that can enable you to buy certain currency pairs. The margin that you will need depends on the leverage that the bank or other financial institutions can offer, and it will represent the guarantee that you need to provide in order to gain control over a certain volume of currency units.

For instance, if you are given a 100:1 leverage, it means that you can control a $100,000 lot or contract with only a $1,000 margin or investment in your forex account. Other forex companies offer lots in smaller sizes to allow new investors to join the forex market. A small lot size will normally allow you to control a $10,000 lot with only a $100 margin or investment.

Let me warn you about forex accounts that provide you with extremely high leverages. These high leverages may permit you to manage a higher volume of currencies in the forex market with a lower margin or investment from your end, but they can also be very risky especially when you start experiencing losses. Because your margin or investment is minimal, you may be tempted to enter positions or transactions that have extreme high risks. You may think that your investment is small and you are willing to lose all of them. That is a good investment mentality, but remember your primary objective in trading forex, which is to earn money in the long run.

Whether you are working with a low or high margin, it is ideal for you to learn how to manage your forex position properly. You need to set "stop-loss" and "target-profit levels" that will enable you to successfully manage the positions that you open. You will learn more about these strategies in the next chapter.

How to Close a Forex Position

When you open a forex position, you can also activate a feature that will allow your account to automatically close the position when it has reached a certain condition that you have specified. These conditions can include target-profit (when your position has reached a certain profit level) or stop-loss (when your position has reached a certain level of loss). You can also choose to manually close your position by logging into your online account or by contacting your broker. When you choose to perform manual closing of your position, you will be subjected to similar conditions that apply when you open a position at market price.

What are Pips and Lots?

As we have mentioned earlier, a point or pip (derived from "Percentage In Point") is the smallest unit of currency movements. A pip represents a 0.0001 variation (either increase or decrease) in currency pairs based on four decimals and a 0.01 variation in currency pairs based on two decimals. For instance, when the price of CHF/USD increases from 1.3740 to 1.3799, it means that the price increased by 59 pips.

Different currency pairs have different pip values which are fundamentally founded on the correlation between the changing currency rates. The computation of a pip is different where EUR is the base currency (such as EUR/USD) compared to a currency pair where EUR is the quote currency (e.g. USD/EUR).

The price movements of currencies are normally gauged by the number of pips. A price movement of one pip is equivalent to a certain amount of profits or losses in real US dollar in each forex trade. Normally, the rate of a pip varies based on the particular currency pairs that are being traded. The rate of a pip will only be similar for currency pairs that have USD as the quote currency (the 2nd currency in the pair). The reason for this is that whatever the base currency is (whether EUR, CHF or AUD), the USD quote currency will always fluctuate at the same rate.

To establish the amount of your profit or loss on a specific trade, you need to first know the rate of the pip and then use that rate to multiply the total number of pips that the currency has moved for or counter to your position. If the price of the base currency increased compared to the price of the quote currency, every pip that the price increased above your original purchase price can be considered as a gain or profit. On the other hand, each pip that price decreased below the original purchase price can be considered as a loss.

It is particularly imperative for you to always remember that if the quote currency is USD (such as CHF/USD), the rate of one pip will always be equal to 0.0001 US dollar or 1/100 of a cent for each US dollar that you trade. This means that the rate of a pip for a standard lot of USD 100,000 is USD 10 and USD 1 for a smaller sized lot of USD 10,000. The rates of a pip for other currency pairs can range from USD 0.00006 to USD 0.00009. This means that a standard lot of USD 100,000 can have a USD 6 to USD 9 pip. Here are a few sample computations that can help you better understand how pips are computed:

US Dollar as the Base Currency

- USD/CHF. If the currency value is equal to 1.1819, the pip value can be computed as 0.0001 divided by 1.1819 or 0.0000846095. Since a standard lot has 100,000 units, the total pip value is equivalent to $8.46 (computed as 0.0000846095 multiplied by 100,000).

- USD/JPY. If the currency value is equal to 92.39, the pip value can be computed as 0.01 divided by 92.29 or 0.0001082368. With a standard lot of 100,000 units, the total pip value is equivalent to $10.82 (computed as 0.0001082368 multiplied by 100,000).

USD Dollar as the Quote Currency

- EUR/USD. If the currency value is equal to 1.2658, the pip value in Euro can be computed as 0.0001 divided by 1.2758 or 0.000078. You can compute for the pip value in US dollar as 0.000078 multiplied by 1.2758 or 0.0001. With a standard lot of 100,000 units, the total pip value is equivalent to $10 (computed as 0.0001 multiplied by 100,000).

- No matter what the base currency is (CHF, AUD, or NZD), the ultimate pip value will always be $10.

The most common order types are market orders and limit orders. You can enter or exit a particular trade position by issuing a "market order" that will allow you to purchase or sell your currencies at present market prices. You need to be extra cautious when issuing market orders, because the forex market can move so fast that the market price at the time your market order is issued and at the actual time of the completion of the buy or sell transaction may vary. This variance is also referred to as "slippage" and can happen in a matter of just a few minutes or even seconds. A slippage can have a potential impact on your transaction, which can result in you losing or gaining a number of pips. Slippage is normally avoided when you transact your forex trading online, because the execution or completion of your market order can be completed instantaneously or in a just a few seconds depending on the speed of your Internet.

You can place a "limit order" which can allow you to automatically buy or sell a particular currency when its price reaches a specific level or limit. For instance, you can place a limit order that will automatically buy a currency when its market price drops below the "limit-order price" that you set, or you can automatically sell a currency when its market price becomes higher than the limit-order price that you set. Slippage risk does not occur with limit orders because your order is technically generated by the computer. Forex traders normally place a limit order when they anticipate that the market price of a currency will eventually recover after a certain economic or political event.

Forex Trading Tools and Strategies

Which is the best trading tool to use?

There are a lot of trading tools that you can use in forex trading. A few of those tools include averages and oscillators. The most common mistake new traders make is to use all the tools at the same time. Many traders feel relaxed when they have all the tools. That way, learning becomes difficult. When you use many tools to trade, you will always want to respond to different signals.

While many signals work well, it is important to know what you are looking for. Sometimes, it can be a bit confusing.

It's okay if you can begin with averages and maybe one oscillator. Try to trade with that strategy and wait to see the results. Make an effort and optimize the parameters. Something else that you should not forget to do is to learn more about the trading tools. Learn all the formulas that come with these tools and try them all.

Which strategy is the best?

As a new trader, chances are that you will ask yourself this question. Many traders will follow a given trend for some time. Others may open a trade position, while some may prefer to trade naked or use fundamental analysis.

Although they are excellent trading strategies, they don't answer the topic question. That said, the best plan should be one that will give you the ability to trade on a higher time frame and make a long-term profit. It doesn't need to be one where you monitor the trend. It can be any other strategy as long as you can make a profit in the long run.

New traders believe that it is a must for them to trade a lower time frame so that they can make a profit. There are more than half of trades controlled by robots on a small time frame. Apart from that, there is that risk to overtrade.

When you trade on a higher time frame, you get enough time to analyze the current situation. That means when you see a move, it is easy to make a high profit. For you to make some good cash trading on a lower time frame, it is advised to invest with high leverage.

Note:

For new traders, it is not right to trade using high leverage.

The Invisible Price Action

In forex trading, everything depends on price. If you choose to add a lot of indicators and other tools, then you may miss on significant price action. For that reason, you should learn to trade on a naked chart from time to time. A naked chart will allow you to be aware of the price movements.

Pivot Points

It is a great trading tool. Pivot points include daily, weekly, and monthly. The best pivot point depends on the major timeframe trading strategy. Of course, the most popular is the daily Pivot Points. You are required to test it by yourself to identify the pivot point that works best for you.

A Strategy Based On Pivots

Pivot points can allow you to build a trading strategy or use them with other trading techniques. Some important points to note about pivots include.

- When the price drops below the pivot line, the line can act as a resistance. On the other hand, when the price moves above the pivot, the line can serve as a support.

High Time Frame Pivots

There are times when it is good to look at the weight incidences for more top time frames. Sometimes, lines from separate pivots maybe near each other. For instance, line R2 can be near line R1. This is important because it allows one to know the point of support that is strong and where you can make profits.

Fibonacci Trading Tools

You will find many trading tools that use Fibonacci. Below is a brief description of some of them.

Fibonacci Retracement

This is the most popular forex trading tool that traders like to use. Fibonacci retracement assists a trader to guess a point a correction may end. In forex trading, an uptrend in price means that there is a pattern of highs. Still, you can have a sequence of high lows or corrections. A correction is when the price rises and suddenly begins to drop. A correction is good because it gives you a chance to open a trade position to make a good profit. In brief, the Fibonacci retracement will allow a trader to predict the point where a correction may stop. As a result, traders have an easy decision to make when they want to enter a trade position.

Fibonacci Expansion

With the following tool, one can predict possible points where there will be high or lows. To achieve this, you must have three locations — the point A and B from the main swing and point C where the correction ends. These points should be enough to allow you to draw a Fibonacci expansion and project possible places for high or low.

Fibonacci Time Zones

The Fibonacci time zones are another exciting tool that traders can use to draw horizontally. You can choose to use it to draw from high to high, high to low or even low to high. Finally, you will get vertical lines that show time and where a change of direction may happen.

Fibonacci Arc

This tool represents places of support and resistance. To draw a Fibonacci arc, you can do it from a high to low or low to high.

Fibonacci Fan

A Fibonacci fan has three diagonal lines. Each line will represent a Fibonacci ratio, and once the price is near the diagonal lines, then that would be the area of support or resistance. Trend lines run between low and high lines. So this tool can be handy when you want to illustrate trends. Furthermore, you can try it out on historical data or test it in your trading. Everything involves choosing the right low and high lines, and you get the best results.

Apart from the tools discussed here, many other tools use Fibonacci numbers. However, the tools presented here are the most popular. Just in case you don't know which one to use, here is a piece of advice. First, start by learning how to use retracement.

Fibonacci Trading in Forex

When you want to draw Fibonacci, you must choose a swing motion and ensure that you select the right one. For that reason, you should understand everything about trends, swings, and price movements.

Let's start with the basics of a price. The first thing you want to know is the direction the price will move. Either the price can move up or down. But what if there is no main trend? Without the main pattern, the price will likely move sideways. Based on forex stats, approximately 30% the price will follow the trend and the remaining percentage the price will run in range. A price that runs in range makes it hard to make a reasonable prediction because there is no clear direction.

How to Recognize a Trend

As a trader, the ability to identify a trend is vital. Sometimes, it is just hard because of the elements of "noise," but there are some hints that you can apply. For example, pay attention to higher highs and higher lows when you look for an uptrend. Similarly, when you are searching for a downtrend, look for the lower highs. Each low will be lower than the previous lower, and each high will be higher than the previous high. Once you have a sequence of lower lows, then you'll have identified a downtrend.

The previous tips aren't the only ways you can use to identify a trend. There are simple tools that define a trend. For example, the moving average. When the moving average rises, there is a high chance that the trend is up. While this method may not be 100% effective, the chances are still good.

Well, what then is Fibonacci trading?

If you know the main trends and how to recognize the current trend, then it is easy to understand Fibonacci trading. In short, Fibonacci trading is a form of trading that uses Fibonacci numbers to predict potential turning points. You will find many tools that use Fibonacci. Each tool is designed to deliver a specific function. Not all tools are the same, and some are more important than others.

Trading with Fibonacci

Up to this point, you have learned a lot of exciting things about Fibonacci tools. But how can one trade with these tools?

While there is no exact answer to this question, Fibonacci tools provide a lot of support and resistance to exit trading points. Well, but how can a trader benefit from it?

The first thing is that a trader should have a trading plan. This trading plan should define how you plan to use the Fibonacci tools. Let your plan have Fibonacci retracement and expansion. Next, set up signals that will remind you when to enter and exit a trading position. The main point is that when the price rises and correction takes place, you must draw levels of retracement.

On the other hand, when prices are close to each other, you can't tell which price will act as a support. That is still okay because you've already defined your signals. In case the price starts to move away from the correction, you'll get your signals.

Same to closing a trading position, you must define which signal that you would like to exit your position. Lastly, your trading plan should include how you want to manage your money. As a trader, your losses should not be more than your profit. Remember. The primary reason why you decided to join forex trading is to make money. So you must keep your losses small. Being a smart trader is the key to forex trading. The bottom line is that you have to practice every time you learn a new idea for you to become successful.

Forex trading is an endless journey that you have to keep testing new strategies and remain open to new ideas. To trade with the Fibonacci tool is a great thing because you already have potential support and resistance levels. Of course, they are possible levels, but history has shown that they work well. So you must find a way that you'll build your trading plan around these levels. If you can learn how to add entry and exit signals properly, you'll be on a great path to success.

Trailing Stop Loss

You can't learn how to trade forex without learning how to hunt stop loss. Stop loss is an excellent forex trading technique. Looks simple but it can help you win big in forex. There are many different ways of trailing stop losses. Some methods are built in the trading platform. That is why you should be keen when it comes to choosing your forex broker.

How can you use a trailing stop loss?

Using a trailing stop loss is simple. First, you must understand how it works. The main advantage that trailing stop loss does to trading is that it helps traders remain in the trend and thus make a huge profit from their open trades.

What is the best setting for trailing stop loss?

You'll find this question frequently asked in forex forums and platforms. But the point is that you must work it out by yourself. A given setting may work well on a pair of currency but fail to work on another currency pair. So traders are advised always to test settings on price history.

It is not hard to trail stop loss. Anyone can do that, but remember that it works well when the trend is solid. Sometimes, the pattern can be strong, or there could be no particular direction at all. However, when there is a range in a move, it can be easy to overtrade and lose your money. For that reason, you must learn to control yourself and stick to your trading plan.

The Timeframe for Trailing Stop Loss

What is the best timeline for hunting stop loss? New traders will ask themselves. Well, time frame depends on your trading strategy. That said traders can hunt stop loss on time frames such as 15m, 30m, and 1h. In this case, the trends can last for some time, and the profit maybe good. If you decide to stoop too low with trailing stop loss such as 1m and 5m, the situation becomes difficult because of the swift movement.

Strategy for Trailing Stop Loss

If you like, you can use only trailing stop loss. However, for the best results, use it with other trading tools. If you want to trade in the same direction as the main trend, focus on integrating trailing stop loss with averages.

Moving Averages in Forex Trading

It is a common problem that investors face. Investors are in the hunt for the best moving averages. But there are better methods that you can use moving average in your trading plan.

For instance, if you randomly pick on ten traders and ask them to come up with their trading system, about 70% of them will use moving average crossovers in their systems. This should not come as a surprise because moving averages is a traditional technical indicator. As time goes by, traders discover complex ways to use it. Also, there are different types of averages but how you use is similar. Crossovers are the best technique to use when the trend is strong. But when the direction isn't clear, the market will move sideways. So it just depends on how you want to use averages.

However, there is a specific way that you can use moving averages. Most traders believe that crossover is the primary method, but that is not the case. Here are ways that you can use averages.

As a Trend Detector

This method will take a longer time frame, and you must monitor the price of your trading position. For instance, if the price eclipses the average, then that is a sign that the entire trend will move up. On the other hand, when the price is below average that means sellers are strong.

What is the direction of average?

You should never ignore the direction where the average is pointing at. For example, when it is pointing up, then there is a high chance that the trend will rise. Alternatively, when it is pointing down, then it means a correction is taking place.

What about price crossing through moving average?

When the price is below average and suddenly changes direction, then it shows that the whole sentiment could be changing.

Moving average as a support or resistance

Traders use some averages like 50, 100, or 200. It is a common thing, and when the price nears these averages, a response is expected. When the price is above average, chances are that support will take place. Alternatively, when the price is below average, and it is moving closer to them, then there is a high chance that the average will act as a resistance.

How many averages should you use?

The number of averages to use depends entirely on the trader and the trading strategy.

Chapter 6: How to Avoid Costly Mistakes

Save yourself some heartache by avoiding these costly mistakes.

> **1.** Don't try to invest more than what you can afford to lose. **Remember, options trading is a risky proposition and if your hunches are wrong or your timing is off it is entirely possible to lose your entire investment. Start off small, no more than 10-15 percent of your**

portfolio should be used for options trading.

2. **Do the proper research.** Don't hurry into an investment because someone told you it was a good idea. Do your own research and make an informed decision before you make a trade.

3. **Adjust your strategy based on market conditions.** No one strategy is going to work in all markets. Keep abreast about what is going on in the economy and the financial world and adapt your trading strategies to match current market conditions.

4. Know your exit strategy before you purchase. **Have a plan and stick to it. Don't let your emotions overrule your rational decisions. Choose your upside and downside exit points as well as your timeframe and don't let the euphoria of making larger profits sidetrack you.**

5. **Don't take on more risk than you are comfortable with.** Every investor has

their own level of risk tolerance. Know your risk comfort level and choose strategies that stay within that territory. You don't want to lose sleep at night wondering if you've made the right investment decisions.

Pricing Principles

Traders may use options to obtain earnings through non-dividend-paying shares to buy a share as well as restrict for its danger. Investors may use options to include influence by having a suitable degree of danger that's genuinely restricted, in addition to industry upward, lower as well as range-bound marketplaces.

In spite of these types of advantages as well as constantly developing quantity (more compared to 15% substance quantity development because 1973), options continue to be within their childhood concerning open public knowing as well as popularity.

Listed here are 10 crucial concepts which beginners to options ought to bear in mind because they make plan for the options industry. Now I am going to discuss these concepts.

Concept 1

Understand the distinction in between utilizing options to get as well as utilizing options to industry: Traders concentrate on the advantages of long-term share possession, and they ought to make use of options to purchase, market, or even safeguard share jobs, in order to improve earnings through share jobs. Think about a good buyer likely to purchase share whenever he or she gets the year-end reward. This particular buyer can purchase 1 phone these days for every 100 gives he or she programs to buy. The phone option is really an agreement that provides the customer to purchase the fundamental share in the hit cost any time before termination day. Basically, it is with regard to having to pay the price of the shares for these days. When the share cost is greater once the buyer gets the actual reward, he then nevertheless can buy the planned-for quantity of gives. With no phone, the amount of gives would need to end up being decreased provided the larger share cost.

Investors, as opposed to traders, tend to be short-term marketplace timers along with small curiosity about having the fundamental share, and they frequently make use of a higher level of influence. Bought options provide investors the possibility of substantial influence along with restricted danger. However, the danger is real. Options may shed 50% or even more of the cost very quickly in the event that the buying prices of the fundamental share techniques the wrong manner. Additionally, out-of-the-money options end useless from termination for any complete lack of the cost compensated, in addition, profits.

Concept 2

Traders who make use of options require a strategy: May the bought option end up being worked out or even offered if it's in-the-money from termination? Protected authors have to know whether they are prepared to market the fundamental share. Otherwise, it is advisable to choose ahead of time from exactly what cost the phone call is going to be repurchased or even folded to an additional option.

Concept 3

Know how as well as the reason why option costs later: Option costs later in a different way compared to share costs, therefore option investors have to strategy in a different way compared to share investors. An average problem through beginners to options is real: "The share proceeded to go upward, however, my personal phone didn't!" Focusing on how costs alter is important to utilizing options effectively.

The worth associated with time provides theoretical ideals of the 50-strike phone from various share costs and various times to termination provided the mentioned presumptions regarding rates of interest, returns as well as volatility. Each one of the series within the desk is really a various share cost, as well as each one of the posts is really a various quantity of times to termination. This discloses 2 essential ideas regarding option costs -- the idea of "delta" which associated with "non-linear period rot.

The idea of "delta" is which for any $1 alter within the fundamental share cost, the worthiness of the phone can change through under $1. Within "The worth of your time, when the share cost increases through $50 to $51 from 3 months, the $50 increases through 50¢. Delta explains the anticipated alter within an option's cost for any $1 alter within the fundamental stock's cost, which means this is referred to as using a delta associated with 0.50.

The desk demonstrates which option costs don't reduce at the exact same price after a while to termination, presuming elements besides time for you to termination stay continuous. Think about the middle strip where the share is $50. Because the time for you to termination reduces through 50% through 3 months to forty-five times, the worthiness from the $50 phone reduces through around 31%

through $3. 20 in order to $2. Twenty-five. It's this that "non-linear period erosion" indicates.

Searching throughout any kind of strip, you will see how the reduction in the passing of your time, so-called period erosion or even theta, differs based on regardless of whether an option is in-the-money, at-the-money or even out-of-the-money.

Concept 4

Option investors require self-discipline within getting earnings as well as deficits: Very first, possess a revenue focus on as well as near or even decrease how big a situation in the event that which cost is actually arrived at. 2nd, possess a stop-loss stage as well as near or even decrease how big a situation from which cost. 3rd, possess a time period limit as well as near or even decrease how big a situation in the event that nor the actual revenue focus on neither the stop-loss stage tends to be arrived at through the finish of times time period.

Concept 5

Don't get freaked away through volatility:
Conceptually, options act like insurance coverage, and also the volatility element in options refers towards the danger element in insurance coverage. It's a key point, however, it's not the only real element. Whilst the idea of volatility isn't without effort apparent in order to beginners, it may be discovered in the event that the first is individual.

Concept 6

It possesses practical anticipation: Learning the actual ideas associated with delta as well as theta (time decay) is definitely an essential action towards the aim of building practical anticipation about how exactly option costs may as well as may not alter as well as just how much revenue possible as well as danger every technique offers.

Concept 7

Buying undervalued options as well as selling over-valued options aren't adequate methods:
"Value" is really a very subjective dedication that each investor should help to make separately. Option

investors should concentrate on their own three-part predict around or even more compared to "value" of the option.

Concept 8

Selling options" isn't a much better technique compared to "buying options": It's a fantasy which 80-90% associated with options end useless. Around 1 / 3, or even 33%, associated with options end useless whilst 10-15% tend to be worked out. The remainder will be shut just before termination. Whilst option composing (selling) could be a prosperous technique, beginners frequently misunderstand this. There's a cause, there's a high quality to take upon much more danger. There isn't any solution to it -- option purchasers spend reasonably limited associated with described danger as well as option retailers get a high quality to take on danger.

Concept 9

Influence is really a double-edged blade: Option investors ought to handle their own funds in a

different way compared to share investors. Your
decision is to buy two hundred gives off the trading
from $50 for each reveal is extremely various how
the option to buy 100 phone trading options from $1
every, despite the fact that each deal includes a
good expense associated with $10, 000, excluding
profits. Usually, options investors may commit an
inferior part of complete funds to every industry.
Option investors, nevertheless, may have much
more open up jobs compared to share investors.

Concept 10

**Create a marketplace predicting method
through beginning little, recognizing earnings
with deficits as well as through operating at a
constant speed:** Investors will be able to clarify
their own trade-selection procedure inside a couple
of phrases. New people can deal which have just
little possible earnings as well as deficits, simply
because this can improve their own likelihood of
sustaining objectivity. Deals should be started and
shut to ensure that the trading rhythm is created.

Almost any person may learn how to work on options trading when they invest a couple of hours in each week on their own method. However, you may invest many years without having learning options.

Discover these types of concepts as well as go one action at any given time. Options tend to be such as levels of the red onion -- there's always something a new comer to discover. Don't grow to become discouraged as well as, more to the point, don't turn out to be more than assured and believe you realize everything simply because you will get burnt.

In Action

Writing A Put Option

Let's assume you are in possession of 100 BHP shares. You are scared that the prices may fall. An idea crops up in your head. You make up your mind to purchase a put option which has a strike price of $25. At any given time until the expiry of the option, you can 'put' your 100 shares to the option seller for $25.

In case there is a fall in price to $24, you will decide to exercise your option since it gives you the chance to sell your number of shares for $25 ($1 above the current market price). On the other hand, if the shares close at a price higher than $25, you won't exercise the option since you could sell for a higher price.

The put option behaves in the same manner as the insurance. The put option buyer pays a premium to lock in a guaranteed price at which they can sell their shares prior to the expiry of the option.

On the other side of the trade, the option buyer buys a premium for the rights to sell the shares as the option seller takes on obligations. The option sellers are obligated to purchase underlying shares from option holders at the strike price. In exchange, the seller gets a premium. The sellers are always assured of compensation when they perceive the trade to be riskier.

Whenever an individual writes an option, they receive money in their trading account after a day. You ought to remember that not unless the option expires, the obligations will not lapse. The time lapse can be up to three months. Nonetheless, the fact that you already have a put option written does not imply you are bound to hold to it until expiry. You have a chance to buy it before the expiry date. In simple terms, once you sell a put option and you get it exercised, you will have the opportunity to buy shares.

Taking an example of the BHP stated above, selling the BHP put option at a strike price of $25 and there was a drop in price to $20 will mean that you will still buy it at $25. It is above the market price and $500 loss is made on one option contract.

Reasons why people write options

People write options as a way to generate income. Options are written over shares. This is done at strike prices where they believe they will not be exercised. The general outlook is that 70% of the option contracts do not get to the level of being exercised.

Probably. You need to get prepared for the contract being exercised. If it does not happen, then, you ought to have funds ready in your account to purchase the stock if it is put across to you.

Writing options are a way of trading. You will expect prices to rise and fall. Options may be sold for no apparent reason than the expectation of buying it at a lowered price in the future. For instance, you may sell an option contract at 80 cents for one share expecting to buy them back at 40 cents a share.

Writing options is a way of giving the players a right to own the underlying shares. Being ready to buy the underlying shares means you are ready to own them. Selling the put options lowers your entry price.

How it works? If a given firm has shares trading at $30 and you want to own them, you will have the privilege of purchasing the shares outright. The other way is selling a put option at a strike price of $30. You may receive 50 cents for every share and end up being exercised. The entry price is at $29.50 per share, which is cheaper as compared to buying the shares directly.

In the event you won't be exercised, you will keep the 50 cents and no ownership of the shares.

Writing strategy for a put option

We write options with the aim of generating income. If not exercised, then it is okay because we will continue writing more to continue the cycle of generating more income. Once an option expires, we move on by writing the next in line.

Never be tempted to sell a put option unless you are prepared to take full ownership of the underlying shares. The stock can be put to you at any given stage. Thus, you should write options that you are willing and happy to own.

On the other side, writing a put option does not directly imply that you must own it until its expiry period. It is a free trading market that entails buyers and sellers. If things do not go as your plan, you will have the chance to buy back a put option to close out your position.

You need to avoid such situation because options are not very liquid as compared to underlying shares.

Meaning you may end up paying more to buy them back. Another reason is about brokerage where you pay for one lot of brokerage in the event you write an option that expires worthless. When you need to buy them back, you will pay a second lot of brokerage as well which becomes a lot of money with time.

The outcomes of this strategy include:

- # You won't be exercised meaning you keep the cash and can repeat the process.
- # You are exercised meaning you will have to buy the shares.

Rules of writing a put option

1. Only write an option at a given strike price that you are willing and ready to pay for the underlying shares. If you are prepared

for $25 a share, do not write a put option
that has a strike price above the $25.

2. Stocks that are more volatile have a higher
   premium on the option. Therefore you are not
   ready to take the risk, then do not write a put
   option over shares of a given company just
   because you expect a larger premium.

3. Option expiry time can range from a month to
   three while others can exceed six, nine or twelve
   months and beyond. Tie value makes the writer
   earn a good-sized premium but more risk is
   involved. Therefore, do not write a put option with
   an expiry date too far away.

4. Write a put option on shares that you are
   willing and happy to own.

The Process of Writing A Call Option for Income

In the previous section, we discussed the two
scenarios that happen when you 'write' a put option.
They all end up to where the share price is when the
option expires. A higher share price over the strike
price means the option is worthless on expiry. If the

share price is lower, the buyer exercises their option at the strike price.

Our aim is to write put options that we are happy to own. Thus, we are ready to own the shares. If we are exercised, we will have the different choices as discussed below. Now that the shares have 'put' to you, what next?

If you wrote a put option and it expires in the money, a broker will notify you that you have been exercised. From here, it won't have a difference to buying shares outright in the market by yourself. You will pay the brokerage fee and settlement will T + 3 just as a normal share transaction.

The ways to take when you get 'put' the shares.

- You may decide to keep the shares. This is so since you wrote put options that you are happy to own. You keep them in your portfolio and manage them just as shares. The put options will earn you a dividend.

- You may decide to sell the shares and make a profit from the proceedings.

- Another way is to keep the shares and write call options over them. Selling call options over the underlying shares 'put' to you allows one to generate cash. Writing call options means you are obligated to sell underlying shares at options strike price if you get exercised.

Before writing call options you ought to understand the tax implications in the event you are exercised. If the options have gained a lot in value with time, you will get profits once you are exercised. You will thus attract capital gains meaning you will be liable to the tax bill.

Writing call options to generate income

Take a situation where you wrote a put at a strike price of $20 and you have been exercised. This means that you have paid $20 for shares which is less the premium you would receive for writing the option.

As a call option writer, you have an obligation to deliver the shares at the strike price if you are exercised. What you ought to do is pick a strike price that you are happy to sell the shares at.

Therefore, if you are not ready to sell the shares below $21, then you are not supposed to choose a call option that has a strike price below $21.

For this example, given that you're happy to sell these shares at $21. You write a call option with a strike price of $21 for which you receive 50 cents per share. If the share price is trading above $21 when the expiry of the option, you'll get exercised. This means that you'll have to deliver your shares for which you'll receive $21. Don't forget that you've already received 50 cents in premium so you're really getting $21.50 for your shares, less any brokerage and other charges.

Now that you have paid $20 per share when the shares were 'put' to you which is less the received premium and now you have received $21.50 per share, less brokerage. Not a bad return.

What about a situation when the share price does not trade above $21? Well, when the option expires, you will be forced to keep the premium and repeat the process again. Another call option indeed. You may sell the next option on expiry of one option. For example, assuming the shares are trading at $20.50, you may sell a $22 call option for which you will receive another different premium. The repeated process is a way to build an income generating stream.

Are there some risks associated with this strategy? With this strategy, you may find yourself buying shares at a price that is higher as compared to the current market price. You need to be aware that some share prices may take a big hit. Reasons can be associated with the given company announcing bad news or the existence of a big fall in the market shareholding.

While you have a choice to buy the option back in the market before it expires, it's vital to know that options are not as liquid as the share market. You will end up paying more just to exit the position. You will find that people write options over the firms they are happy to own for dividend incomes and at a price that they are willing and ready to pay.

A deviation on the theme

In the strategy above, we will write call options on shares if they happen to be 'put' to us. Instead of writing a put option and waiting for it to be exercised on you, you may decide buy the shares outright in the market and then write a call option over them at the same time. This is a' buy/write' strategy.

For example, you may buy a company's shares trading at $8 and then write a $9 call option over them. If you don't get exercised, you will retain the premium. If you are exercised, you lock in a profit from the share sale, plus the premium you've already received.

Let's look at an example. We use a random company called ABC Corporation.

Step 1

After having a thorough analysis, you have resolved to but shares for ABC Corp. since you are happy to own them. They are trading at $11 but your intention is to buy when the price is $10.

Action to take: You will write a put option with a strike price of $10 and get a premium of 30 cents a share. On one contract, if you get 'put' shares, you will be needed to pay up a total of $1,000 ($10 per share multiplied by one contract –equivalent to 100 shares).

If you traded out the put option, you would get 30 cents per share, meaning you will get $30 for the contract. If you are not exercised, you will keep the premium, less any charges including brokerage. You will generate more income by ensuring that you repeat the process again given that you are happy to own the shares at the strike price.

If you are exercised, you will buy the shares in ABC Corp. at $10, irrespective of the price it is trading at. The operational entry price is now $9.70 ($10 strike price less the 30 cents earned in premium).

Step 2

If you have 'put' your shares, you may earn additional income writing a call option over them.

If ABC Corp. shares are currently trading at $10, then the action to be taken is as follows. Write an $11 call option. Here, you get 30 cents per share. Given a situation does not trade above $11 and you are not exercised, you will keep the premium. You can opt to repeat the process. You will write the call option at a strike price that you are willing and prepared to sell the shares at. If they trade at a price above the $11 strike price and in the eventuality that you are exercised, you will sell the shares at a price that you are happy with.

Step 3

If the call option you sold over ABC Corp. is exercised and you now own the shares (and received the strike price as well), you may decide to repeat the procedure from step 1.

Chapter 7: Trading Tips for Intermediate Traders

1. Trading Forex Options Tips for Intermediate Traders

As a trader, the more experience you gain, the more variables seem to be at play. Some of these may improve your performance while some may not. In most cases, these just add layers of complications and are mostly settings and indicators.

It is advisable to focus on factors that actually support your trades and enable you to perform and increase your profitability. Here we shall examine a couple of tips that will help you become a better and more successful trader. These tips are directed at intermediate traders even though others too could benefit from these tips.

One of the most crucial factors in Forex trading is consistency. If you wish to develop and become a successful Forex trader, then you should be consistent. Being consistent is essential, yet most people are not even consistent in their lives. Certain platforms provide systems with a set of reasonable rules. Following these rules helps traders to perform well, excel, and become successful.

You need to keep in mind that Forex trading is all about taking risks. However, these are measured and calculated risks rather than blind groping in the dark. As a Forex trader, you are mostly a risk manager, so you need to be totally vigilant as you place traders and invest monies in your trades. There are a couple of things you need to focus on once the trades are entered.

Find triggers

One of the first things that you need to do after placing a trader is to dial down for triggers. This is one way of managing risks and lowering your risks. When you lower down your risks, you improve your chances of success, and as such, you can go for a great size.

To achieve this successfully, you will need a chart that makes use of Fibonacci symmetry and retracement. Such a chart will have a slanted line and an upper line. Find the upper line because it is the trigger line. This line basically indicates or points to the nearest level that has to be broken just so you may continue with the upward trend.

As an intermediate Forex trader, you should endeavor to identify a pathway to enter the trade at a point that is nearer to the market's determined turning point. In order to find such an entry point, you will basically do what is known as down dialing.

With a good chart, you should be able to trade with a risk profile of close to 78 pips. At such a level, the price will begin to showcase another preferred entry point. At this stage, you will want to enter the trade at the 51 pips level with a buffer of about 5 pips. The most likely scenario is that the trend will begin an upward climb. What this will have achieved is reducing our risk profile by 50% and allows you better performance with higher performance at the end of it.

Scale your trades for risk

As a trader, the bottom line is always driven by the desire to be profitable. This is what you will achieve by following this specific tip. Now, we will identify another entry point known as level 2.

At this point, we will enter at 51 pips. As a trader, when you scale out to half of your position, it will enable you to have free trade. Therefore, should the price retrace back to the beginning then we can only breakeven even in the worst-case scenario. Other than that, your trades will only be profitable from here. You can add a couple of extra pips so that if your trades have to stop, then you will still have had free trade.

Such an approach is excellent especially for traders who are unable to watch the market or make adjustments to their stop-loss systems. As an intermediate trader, you should have sufficient experience to set up a trade then forget all about it, so the price action determines the trade without the need for regular interventions.

We can be wrong sometimes

By now we know that even the best analysis does not always win. There is never a 100% guarantee that the market will move as predicted. It is, therefore, the reason why you can take the risk out of the trade.

Go for profits

As an intermediate trader, you have learned all about setting up trades, learning how to enter and exit trades, how to identify great opportunities, how to read charts and all that. By this stage now, you should focus on profits. This is because we learn all this technical stuff in order to eventually learn how to be profitable. There are different ways of going about this. There are generally two great ways of doing this. These are using moving averages and using price structure.

You can also keep close track of your stop by using one of the moving averages. Using such approaches for profits will help remove emotions from your trades and enable you to trade with confidence and thereby become profitable.

Effective indicators that you should be aware of

As a Forex trader, you are likely to encounter plenty of various trading methods. Making use of only four chart indicators is possible. These can help you with almost all Forex trading opportunities. These chart indicators are the MACD indicator, the Moving Average, Stochastic, and the RSI. As a trader, you will receive Forex indicators and free reinforcement tools to use each trading day.

Use a simple strategy

A lot of traders tend to complicate matters, especially in their early trading days. As an intermediary trader, you should try as much as possible to avoid complicating things. Instead, you should focus more on simplifying your trades so that everything is clear and all that you do must have a clearly defined purpose.

Plenty of traders think that complicated trading strategies with plenty of variables perform better yet the main focus should be on simple strategies that will have a direct bearing on profitable trades. Also, strategies that are simple and straightforward have less stress and allow for fast reactions should this be necessary. As an intermediate trader, you need to work on coming up with simple strategies that are effective and will help you identify trades.

2. Tips for Intermediate Futures Options Traders

As a futures trader, you should make sure that you understand very clearly what a short position is and a long position is. There are plenty of novice traders who believe that you only make money or are profitable when markets are on an upward trend.

However, you need to understand that futures' trading constitutes a lot more than just following the upward market trend. You also should know by now that as a futures trader you can benefit greatly when you focus on asset types that have attained a climax and are close to failure.

As a trader, anytime that you wage your money against an asset, then you will be said to be selling it short. Selling an asset short simply means that you will engage your broker and purchase the rights to access the asset with the hopes of selling it back later once it becomes profitable. Using this analogy, we can purchase apples at the market for $1 each and then selling them back at $2 each making a profit of $1.

In real life, this $1 can be exponentially multiplied to earn you large sums of money. This is the way futures markets work. You stand to make large sums of money from simple trades.

Long positions

As a futures trader, you are ready to invest your funds in a particular asset when you take a long position in it. In this situation, you will only benefit from this position when the price of the asset rises. As a futures trader, you need to be able to determine whether and when an asset is likely to rise in price. This determination requires you to learn about the fundamentals of the asset. For instance, how is the supply and demand in the market? Being able to answer such questions with a high level of accuracy will enable you to decide whether to invest in it or not.

Basically, each asset market has its own rules that help interested parties, including traders, to provide intrinsic value as well as the determination of momentum, both negative and positive. The Central Bank is the premier institution when it comes to currency, so currency traders need to take note of the policies and statements released by this institution.

In this instance, currency fluctuations sometimes depend on interest rates. If you anticipate a rate hike, then it is advisable to go long on the specific currency. Higher interest rates should provide a suitable incentive to hold long an asset. This way, there will be increasing demand in the currency, and you will be able to eventually sell at a great price and make lots of profits.

When it comes to stocks and other instruments, it is corporations that drive their value. For instance, the earnings report will determine the value of a company's stock in the short and long terms. Earnings reports are often released quarterly. During these events, company executives reveal their earnings for the past three months as well as their forecasts for the future. Therefore, if a company announces a reduction in production, closure of a store or plant and so on, then you should assume a long position. The reason is that reduced production will very likely result in higher prices within a couple of months.

Short position

When it comes to short positions, there are plenty of similar factors compared to long positions at play but in reverse. Therefore, factors or elements that cause you to choose a long position will, in reverse, determine a short position. For instance, if you are interested in currency and there are signs of reduced inflation, then you may want to take a short position on the currency.

Basically, when there are signs of declining inflation, central banks may decide to lower interest rates in order to provide a stable financial position in the markets. On the other hand, when interest rates are high, then as a futures trader, you will want to take the path that all other futures traders do. When interest rates are high, products and services are generally expensive for the consumer.

Costly products mean lower sales figures, and this will mean reduced incomes for corporations and so on. As such, it will be appropriate for futures traders to sell short because of the high-interest rates. Some of the instruments that can be sold include shares and stock indices. Commodities markets and their instruments also operate in the same manner. When there are high-interest rates at play, the markets tend to experience low demand. Commodities such as gold and oil will then most likely begin selling short at the markets.

Basically, it is advisable to have a good idea regarding factors that are actually negative and which ones are considered positive especially with regards to your preferred asset. This way, you can do your research and analysis to determine if you are to sell an asset or buy.

Intermediate futures trading

It is often difficult for traders with small accounts to make any significant gains in the futures market. As an intermediate trader, you do not need to be too concerned about this. This is because you can use leverage to overcome your small account size challenges.

Leverage provides an effective pathway that enables you to capitalize effectively on your positions. Leverage also provides a reliable pathway that will enable you to increase your profit potential as you maximize on your positions in the trade. This means that you will be able to leverage in a manner that allows you to profit in numerous ways not otherwise possible.

Leverage can help you maximize your gains. However, be extremely cautious because leverage can also compound your losses should you incur any. It is possible that your analysis could travel in the wrong direction. When this happens, you could incur some losses, and these could have an impact on your account. You could, for instance, receive what is known as a margin call. When this happens, you will be required to fund your trading account. Should you not be able to fund your account due to losses, then it will be shut down.

Chapter 8: Dos and Don'ts of Forex Trading

Dos of forex trading

Research

The very first thing to understand is the research that you need to conduct on the topic. You have to understand everything that there is to about it in order to make the right investment choices. This book will act as your one true forex guide no doubt, but you must not limit yourself to just the information that is provided in it. You should turn to other sources as well and increase your knowledge as much as possible. Just ensure that you are turning to reliable sources such as reliable websites and other book publications that will provide you with the correct information.

Terminologies

The next step is for you to get acquainted with the different terminologies that are used in forex trading. These terminologies are an important part of the trade. Many of your fellow traders will use these words, and you have to understand what they are saying. You should not take it for granted and think that you will understand the words as and when you go. You have to put in the efforts and by heart the different words if possible. You will be able to trade easily when you are acquainted with these words, and your trade will start to flow like water.

Gain ratio

You should always keep track of your profits. If you have made a lot of investments, then you should maintain a book and record all the different profits that you have gained from each of the different investments. You have to be abreast with all the income that is coming in. Remember to always set a specific limit on all your currencies. As soon as the limit is reached and you have earned the desired profit, you should immediately sell it. Don't wait on it for too long as the market can be quite volatile and the prices might start to dip. Calculate the profit margin at the very behest and sell the currency as soon as the limit is reached.

Strategies

The next thing is to understand the different strategies that are employed in forex trading. You have to understand how to calculate the fundamental analysis, the technical analysis and also the sentimental analysis. All three are important aspects of forex trading, and you have to understand each in detail in order to make the most of your trading. You will see that it is easy for you to choose the currencies that you can invest in when you do the fundamental and technical analysis of the stocks. You can go through how each one is calculated in order to effectively conduct it on a daily basis. Don't take it lightly as these calculations are what will help you make the right choice.

Software

You have to make use of the latest prediction software to understand how the prices of the currencies will move. The software will give you a near guarantee prediction, which will be enough for you to make your choice. But you must not over-rely on the software. It might end up giving a near accurate reading or something that is completely off. You have to be prepared for either result.

Calculate loss

When you gain profits, it is obvious that you will also suffer loss. You have to calculate both your profits and your losses in order to understand whether it is a lucrative deal for you or not. Keep track of all your losses and also ensure that you try to reduce it as much as possible. That is only possible if you make the right decisions and invest in the right currencies. Don't get over enthusiastic and start investing in the wrong stocks just to cover up a bad one. Take it slow, and you will be able to reverse the damage.

Operation

The next thing is to understand how you can operate the software. You should understand how to access the website, how you can log in, look for the currencies, understand the bid/ask ratio, etc. All of this will be a bit difficult for all those that are not accustomed to the practice of buying and selling stocks. If you are new to it, then you have to take the help of an expert to understand all of these and carry them out smoothly.

Firm head on shoulders

Remember to always have a firm head on your shoulders. Don't make the mistake of making impulsive decisions. You should not take it to heart if you suffer a loss. You have to instead think of it as a learning curve and move on. There is really no point in taking offense for an unforeseen circumstance. You have to remain confident and continue trading. You will be able to cover a loss, no matter how big and move ahead.

Fundamental and technical analysis

You have to learn to calculate the fundamental and technical analysis. You must use it to find the best currencies to trade in.

Don'ts of forex trading

No planning

As an investor, you should always work with a plan. Those that don't work with a plan will end up getting lost. It is the same as a tourist going to a new place without a map. He will obviously get lost. So, in order to avoid such a situation, you have to work as per a plan and avoid falling into unnecessary traps. You will be better prepared to take quick decisions. Now say for example there is an opportunity for you to buy a lucrative pair. But just as soon as you buy it you hear that the currency value is going to drop. Here, you have not planned the buying, and so your investment has the chance of going bad. So, to avoid any such issues you should have a plan in place.

Short selling

The next don't of forex is selling short. Selling short refers to you settling for a loss in order to quickly sell off a certain currency. This will only cause you to undergo unnecessary loss. Short selling is not advisable for any trader unless the situation absolutely calls for it. But situations rarely arise, and so, you have to remain patient and wait for the prices to rise again before selling off your currencies.

Relying too much

Do not make the mistake of over-relying on someone as that will only end badly for you. You have to make your own choices and remain confident of them. It can be your broker or just a friend or family member. They might give you the wrong advice, and you might end up suffering losses. Before you make any kind of investment, you have to compulsorily do a personal inspection and only then invest in the currencies. It is after all your money that is being invested, and so, you have to be careful about it.

Depending on luck

Do not over depend on your luck. Some people make the mistake of depending too much on their luck and end up making mistakes. Maybe you did well at the beginning owing to beginners luck, and the same might not continue for long. You have to try and remain as practical and logical as possible when you invest in the stock market, and the same extends to your forex investments.

Picking extremes

Some people make the mistake of picking two extreme currency pairs. That will seem like a good idea but really is not. Say for example you pick a strong currency like the Dollar and a weak one like the Indian rupee. You will have the chance to make a big profit from these no doubt, but you have to calculate the risk that such an investment might put forth. The currency market is extremely volatile, and you have to account for all those things that can go wrong. Being prepared is key, and you have to be as careful as possible while choosing your currency pairs. Stick with the ones that are working well for you and don't experiment too much with it.

Getting emotional

Some traders make the mistake of getting very emotional with their currencies and getting too attached. If that happens, then you will not be able to sell it on time and remain with a profit. You have to trade with your mind and not from your heart. If you think that that is what is happening with you, then you must take stock of the situation at the earliest and fix the problem. Think of currencies as nothing but money making instruments and not any kind of person. Even if a certain currency has worked well for you in the past and is now doing badly, then you have to let go of it and move to another one.

Expecting too much

Do not expect overnight riches with your forex investments. That has never happened and never will. You have to have practical and reasonable expectations if you wish to make it big in the world of forex. Try to remain as practical as possible and think before reaching any consensus.

These form the various dos and don'ts of forex that you have to follow if you wish to make it big.

Conclusion

If you are new to options trading, then you will need all the advice, tips and guidance necessary, in order to trade successfully. It is, however, first recommended that you understand a concept, apply it and master it then add more knowledge. This is a much better and more successful strategy. Here are some helpful tips and advice that should guide you as you trade online in options.

1. The price of any stock can move in 3 basic directions

These directions are up, down and no movement at all. Depending on the kind of call that you have, you can leverage from this movement to make a profit or at least avoid incurring losses.

Plenty of first-time traders and investors assume that prices of securities will go either up or down. However, this is a wrong school of thought because sometimes there is no movement at all in the price of stocks and shares. This is a very important fact in the world of options trading.

Plenty of real-life, practical examples show a particular stock or share did not move significantly for quite a lengthy period. For instance, the KOL share traded within a $4 range for a total of 23 days. If you had invested money in either a call option or a put option through this stock, you would have lost money.

According to seasoned traders, chances of making a profit with a call or put option are hardly ever 50% but only 33%. This is likely due to the fact that stock price movements are random. You will eventually realize that 33% of the time, stocks rise, 33% of the time they dip in price and another 33% of the time they stay the same. Time will more often be your worst enemy if you have a long put or call option.

A purchase of a call option is usually with the hope that prices will go up. In the event that prices do rise, then you will make a profit. At other times the prices will remain the same or even fall. In such events, if you have an out-of-the-money call, the option will most likely expire, and you will lose your investment. In the event that the price remains stagnant and you have an in-the-money option, then you will at least recoup some of the money you invested.

There will be times when frustrations will engulf you. This is when you just sit and watch prices start to skyrocket just a couple of weeks after the options you purchased had expired. This is often an indicator that your strategy was not on point and you did not give it sufficient time. Even seasoned traders sometimes buy call options that eventually expire in a given month and then the stocks prices rise sharply in the following month.

It is therefore advisable to purchase a longer-term call option rather than one that expires after a single month. Now since stocks move in 3 general directions, it is assumed that close to 70% of options traders with long call and put options suffer losses. On the other hand, this implies that 70% of option sellers make money. This is one of the main reasons why conservative options traders prefer to write or sell options.

2. Before buying options look at the underlying stock's chart

Basically, you want to find out as much information as possible about the performance and worth of an underlying stock before investing in it.

You should, therefore, ensure that you take a serious look at the chart of the stock. This chart should indicate the performance of the stock in the last couple of days. The best is to look at a stock's performance in the last 30 and 90 days. You should also take a look at last year's performance.

When you look at the charts, look at the movement of the shares and try note any trends. Also, try and observe any general movement of the shares. Then answer a couple of questions. For instance, is the stock operating within a narrow range or is it bending upwards or downwards? Is this chart in tandem with your options trading strategy?

To identify the trend of a particular stock, try and draw a straight line along in the middle of the share prices. Then draw a line both above and below so as to indicate a channel of the general flow of the share.

Chart readings and buying call options

Let us assume you wish to invest in a call option. Then you should ask yourself if the stock price is likely to rise and why. If you think the stock will rise and trade at a higher level, then you may be mistaken, unless something drastic happens or new information becomes evident. New information can be a shareholders meeting, impending earnings announcement, a new CEO, product launch and so on.

If there is a chart showing the presence of support at lower prices and stock prices fall to that level, then it may be advisable to buy call options. The call option will be a great bet when prices are down because prices will very likely head back up. However, never allow greed to occupy your mind. When you see a profit, take and do not wait too long.

Chart readings and buying put options

Now supposing the stock chart indicates a solid resistance at a higher price. If the stock is beginning to approach this higher level, then it is possible that the price might begin to move in that direction as well. So as the price moves, expect to gain small but significant profits. Avoid greed so that anytime the stock price falls simply move in and make some money.

Chart readings for purchase of call and put options

Now, if your chart readings indicate that the shares are within the lower levels of its range, then it is likely that daily changes in price will send it towards the middle of the range. If this is so, then you should move in and make a profit as soon as the price tends upwards. Even minor profits such as buying at $1 and selling at $1.15 means a 15% profit margin.

3. Find out the break-even point before buying your options

Now you need to identify a call option that you wish to invest in, especially after studying its performance on the market. Before buying, however, you should work out the break-even point. In order to find this break-even point, you will have to consider things such as the commissions charged and the bid spread.

It is very important that you are positive the underlying stock of your options will move sufficiently so as to surpass the break-even point and earn a tidy profit. You should, therefore, learn how to work out the break-even point in options trade.

Calculating the break-even point

As an options trader, you need to know how to calculate and find the break-even point. In options trading, there are basically 2 break-even points. With short term options, you need to make use of the commission rates and bid spread to work out the break-even point. This is if you intend to hold on to the options until their expiration date.

Now if you are seeking short term trade without holding on to the options, then find out the difference between asking price and bid price. This difference is also known as the spread.

4. Embrace the underlying stock's trend

As an investor and trader in options, you need to consider the trend of the underlying stock as your friend. This means that you should not fight it. Basically, if the stock price is headed upwards, you should find a strategy that is in tandem with this movement. If you oppose it, you are unlikely to win.

Similarly, if the stock is on a downward trend, then do not oppose this movement but try and find a strategy that will accommodate this trend. You need to understand however that this saying is intended to guide you but is not necessarily a rule. This means you apply it even while you consider all other factors. For instance, the major news may have an immediate effect on the price trend of a stock or shares.

As a trader, you should learn to jump successfully on a trend and follow the crowds rather than go to extremes and oppose it. Most amateurs who see an upward trend often think the stock is about to level out. However, the reality is that the momentum is often considered a great thing by seasoned traders. Therefore, do not try and oppose the trend because you will surely lose. Instead, try and design a strategy that will accommodate the trend. In short, the trend is always your friend, do not resist as momentum is great.

5. Watch out for earnings release dates

Call and put options are generally expensive with the price increases significantly if there is an earnings release announcement looming. The reason is that the anticipation of very good or very bad earnings report will likely affect the stock price. When this is an underlying stock in an options trade, then you should adjust your trades appropriately.

Once an earnings release has been made, then options prices will fall significantly. You need to also watch out very carefully for this. The prices will first go up just before the earnings are released and then fall shortly thereafter. It is also possible for call options prices to dip despite earnings announcements. This may happen if the earnings announced are not as impressive as expected.

As an example, stocks such as Google may rise insanely during the earnings announcement week only to dip significantly shortly thereafter. Consider Apple shares that were trading at $450 at the markets. Call options with Apple as the underlying stock were trading at $460. However, the market had targeted a price of $480 within 3 days, which did not happen. This costs investors money. Such underlying assets are considered volatile due to the high increase in price, rapid drop shortly thereafter and a related risk of losing money.